Teaching Mission
in a Global Context

Teaching Mission in a Global Context

Edited by
Patricia Lloyd-Sidle and Bonnie Sue Lewis

Geneva Press
Louisville, Kentucky

Book design by Sharon Adams
Cover design by Rohani Design
Cover illustration by Rohani Design

First edition
Published by Geneva Press
Louisville, Kentucky

This book is printed on acid-free paper that meets the American National Standards Institute Z39.48 standard. ∞

PRINTED IN THE UNITED STATES OF AMERICA

01 02 03 04 05 06 07 08 09 10 — 10 9 8 7 6 5 4 3 2 1

Library of Congress Cataloging-in-Publication Data

Teaching mission in a global context / edited by Patricia Lloyd-Sidle and Bonnie Sue Lewis.—1st ed.
 p. cm.
 Includes bibliographical references.
 ISBN 0-664-50154-0 (pbk.)
 1. Missiologists—United States. 2. Presbyterian Church—Missions—Study and teaching—United States. I. Lloyd-Sidle, Patricia. II. Lewis, Bonnie Sue.

BV2072 .T43 2001
266'.0071—dc21   00-052108

Contents

Acknowledgments   vi

Contributors   vii

Part I Jumping in Feet First   **1**

A Journey between Friends: An Introduction   3
Bonnie Sue Lewis

Feet First: How Practices Have Shaped My Theology
    of Evangelism and Mission   8
Frances S. Adeney

Part II Mission at the Margins   **23**

Mission at the Borders: Developing Our Mission Theology
    and Praxis through Biography and Testimony   25
Carlos F. Cardoza-Orlandi

From Missionary to Missiologist at the Margins:
    Three Decades of Transforming Mission   40
Sherron K. George

Part III Mission in a Pluralist Society   **55**

Among the Believers: Muslims and Christians in the *Dar al-Islam*   57
Stanley H. Skreslet

Reconciliation: A Vision of Christian Mission   69
Syngman Rhee

Toward the Development of a New Christian Missiological Identity   79
Marsha Snulligan Haney

Unfinished Journey: My Pilgrimage in Mission   93
Philip L. Wickeri

Part IV Mission as Church-with-Others   **109**

Asian Spirituality and Christian Mission   111
Scott W. Sunquist

Learning to Listen   124
Bonnie Sue Lewis

Growing Evangelizing Churches   134
Darrell L. Guder

Glossary of Terms   149

Acknowledgments

The author of Ecclesiastes had it right: "Two are better than one, because they have a good reward for their toil. For if they fall, one will lift up the other; but woe to one who is alone and falls and does not have another to help" (Ecc. 4:9, 10). Editing a book is never an easy project, but woe to the one who has to do it alone! We are extremely grateful that from its inception, this book was a joint effort between a seminary professor in Dubuque, Iowa, and a staff member of the Worldwide Ministries Division of the Presbyterian Church (U.S.A.) in Louisville, Kentucky. Together we have planned, prayed, and put into your hands what we hope will be an asset to your understanding of mission as it is being taught in our Presbyterian seminaries in this new millennium. This has been an undertaking that would have folded long ago had God not paired us up to share the responsibilities, burdens, and joys of this project. Thanks be to God for my partner in this work!

Thanks must also be extended to each of the contributors to this collection. Though it focuses on feet, this is a book only made possible by the labors of many hands! We want to thank each professor who took time out of extremely busy and active lives to reflect upon what has shaped his or her teaching on mission and to share that with others. We believe that the church has benefitted not only from the dedication of these professors to God's mission in the world, but by the passion for God and God's mission that they are passing to future generations of church pastors.

Special thanks go to Scott Sunquist, Sherron George, Michael Boyland, and Tim Carriker who, as we sat over our morning lattes that June morning in 1999, dreamed up the idea of this project and then encouraged us to run with it. Bradley Longfield, Dean of the University of Dubuque Theological Seminary, gave generously of his time to read various parts of this manuscript. Thank you for your editorial gifts, your patience, and your encouragement.

We are grateful to the Worldwide Ministries Division for nurturing the community of Presbyterian mission professors and to Geneva Press for its enthusiastic support of this project.

Bonnie Sue Lewis
Dubuque, Iowa

Patricia Lloyd-Sidle
Louisville, Kentucky

Contributors

Frances S. Adeney
William A. Benfield Jr. Associate Professor of Evangelism and Global Mission
Louisville Presbyterian Theological Seminary

Carlos F. Cardoza-Orlandi
Associate Professor of World Christianity
Columbia Theological Seminary

Sherron K. George
Associate Professor of Evangelism and Missions
Austin Presbyterian Theological Seminary

Darrell L. Guder
Peachtree Professor of Evangelism and Church Growth
Columbia Theological Seminary

Marsha Snulligan Haney
Associate Professor of Missiology and Religions of the World
Johnson C. Smith Seminary
A Constituency of the Interdenominational Theological Center

Bonnie Sue Lewis
Assistant Professor of Mission and Native American Christianity
University of Dubuque Theological Seminary

Syngman Rhee
Director of Asian American Ministry and Mission Center and
Distinguished Visiting Professor of Evangelism and Mission
Union Theological Seminary, Richmond

Stanley H. Skreslet
Associate Professor of Christian Mission
Union Theological Seminary, Richmond

Scott W. Sunquist
W. Don McClure Associate Professor of World Mission and Evangelism
Pittsburgh Theological Seminary

Philip L. Wickeri
Flora Lamson Hewlett Professor of Evangelism and Mission
San Francisco Theological Seminary

PART I

Jumping in Feet First

A Journey between Friends

An Introduction

BONNIE SUE LEWIS

*I*t began very casually over coffee during the 1999 annual meeting of the American Society of Missiology/Association of Professors of Mission in Techny, Illinois, a suburb of Chicago. We were reflecting on what it means to be teaching mission today in the ten seminaries of the Presbyterian Church (U.S.A.). As we talked about the challenges of teaching local and global mission in the context of a complex, pluralistic, postmodern, and post-Christian world, we realized that God seems to have begun a "new thing" in most of our seminaries by bringing a whole new generation of professors into them.

The relatively new faculties in missiology were schooled in doing mission during the last decades of the twentieth century, when a decided paradigmatic shift in the understanding of mission took place. As mission workers themselves, most of the seminary professors have experienced the dramatic change of Christian churches growing fastest in the southern and eastern hemispheres, of most missionaries coming from churches that were themselves missionized only a century ago, and of mission becoming the church with others in a post-Christendom world. From China, Singapore, Egypt, and Brazil, among others, the missiologists of today have learned what it means to do mission at the margins of society, to practice mission in reverse, to meet the challenge of witnessing to Christ with humility and purpose where Christian communities are in the minority. In the terms of missiologist David Bosch, these experiences have not only transformed mission, but have transformed the professors who now teach mission.

This is the story of those professors. The autobiographical accounts presented here reveal a breadth of mission experience and involvement, a depth of theological education, and an evangelical commitment to God that heralds a new vision for mission as we enter a new millennium. The narratives reflect pilgrimages in mission and how those pilgrimages have shaped the professors and how they now teach mission. What they have learned about God and God's mission (the *missio Dei*) is now being passed on to seminarians across the United States. All but two of the ten Presbyterian seminaries are represented here (Princeton and McCormick seminaries are both searching for new missiologists as this goes to press). It seems fitting that one of these mission professors, Syngman Rhee of North Korea and a professor at Union Theological Seminary, Richmond, now leads the denomination as the moderator of the 212th General Assembly. God indeed is doing a new thing.

Common themes such as faith, community, hospitality, and transformation emerge from the collection of ten stories in this volume. They all seem to revolve around feet. Feet are a fitting image of mission today. As the Word of God is a lamp to our feet and a light to our path (Ps. 119:105), mission is informed by the *missio Dei*—it is God's mission and we must begin with knowing God. All of these accounts are first and foremost a collection of faith journeys. They are a testimony of how God has spoken through his Word, through his Son, Jesus Christ, and through his church empowered by the Holy Spirit. They are about learning to listen to God and to God's people.

These are also stories about stepping out in faith. As the prophet Habakkuk promised, "The Sovereign LORD is my strength; he makes my feet like the feet of a deer," enabling us to go surefooted where God leads (Hab. 3:19, NIV). Sometimes this means going "feet first" into places and situations we have not dreamed of, walking alongside others on the journey of faith. Often it means walking with the marginalized, bridging worlds separated by hatred and distrust, learning how to be the church in the midst of those of other faiths or persuasions. We must trust the One who calls and sends, as well as the ones we are called to serve among.

God chooses community to extend the kingdom. Isaiah exclaimed, "How beautiful on the mountains are the feet of those who bring good news" (Isa. 52:7, NIV). These testimonies witness to the power of the whole church bringing the whole gospel to the whole world. Hospitality and humility are at the heart of many of these stories. Jesus washed the feet of the disciples and told them—and us—to do likewise (John 13:14). How often the missionary's feet are the ones that are washed as he or she experiences mission in reverse. Many of the professors' reflections speak of the transformative power of being ministered to even as they ministered. Mission is as much about receiving as giving.

The original title of Frances Adeney's submission, "Feet First: How Practices Have Shaped My Theology of Mission," captured our imaginations and provided the framework for this collection of autobiographical articles from the seminary professors of mission. Adeney, a professor at Louisville Seminary, leads off with a story about how her work as a Presbyterian mission coworker in Indonesia was shaped by the various faith communities of which she was a part. Her theology of mission comes out of her experiences of God and God's mission in several different contexts.

Having set the tone with Adeney's narrative, we become more specific in the next two articles, which tell about what it means to do "mission at the margins." Carlos Cardosa-Orlandi of Columbia Seminary shares what it is like to "live at the border" as an evangelical, third world (or two-thirds world) Christian missiologist. To be in mission here means dealing with multiple realities, conflict, and pain. It also means that God is very real and very present.

Sherron George of Austin Seminary writes from the perspective of more than twenty years as a Presbyterian mission worker in Brazil. Her identity with the Brazilian church not only transformed her into a "marginal, bicultural Christian . . . of the global faith community," but led her to believe that mission itself must be transformed, that the church must focus upon doing mission in mutuality and solidarity with others. It must work among and identify with the marginalized in "bold humility" to be the church in mission. True mission most often takes place at the margins.

The second set of narratives revolves around the theme of mission in a pluralist society. Stan Skreslet begins this section with his account of living and working among Muslims and Christians in the Middle East over the past twenty-five years. In his experience, this part of the world is a place where "a society's whole life [is] richly permeated with religious language and infused with the conviction of faith that yearns to be shared." Both Muslims and Christians taught him the value and the way of witnessing freely to one's faith while building relationships with one another.

Syngman Rhee's focus on reconciliation comes within the context of his own experience as a North Korean refugee. The son of a Christian minister and the grandson of a "Bible woman," Rhee's fascinating story of a life caught between the two Koreas is a timely one as these two countries begin to talk of reunification. Rhee calls upon the church to lead the way toward reconciliation, a mission theme he has championed as moderator of the General Assembly.

Marsha Snulligan Haney, of Johnson C. Smith Seminary, also explores what it means to do mission in Christian and Muslim contexts. From her experiences within the Reformed and Black Church traditions and as a

Presbyterian mission worker in Sudan and Cameroon, Snulligan Haney emphasizes the importance of incarnational ministry and faithful witness to the gospel in cross-cultural encounters. She is committed to contextualization, interfaith dialogue, and global theological education, and she affirms the diversity of cultures within the Presbyterian Church and the church at large.

Philip Wickeri's narrative ends the section on mission in a pluralist society. From his twenty-three years as a Presbyterian mission worker in postcolonial Asia, a period of adversity and amazing church growth, Wickeri claims he learned what the church was all about. It was "one of the many gifts Asia gave to me." Wickeri, of San Francisco Theological Seminary, sees mission as "a journey between friends," because we are called as "coworkers in God's mission to the world."

Although multiple themes are found within each of these narratives that make it difficult to place many of them in only one category, the final section of this book focuses on the stories of those professors that emphasize mission as the church with others. It is an emphasis on working with God and with others in the local congregation to witness to the love of God in Christ.

Scott Sundquist of Pittsburgh Seminary draws from his long teaching experience in Asia to share what he has learned about being the church from his "Asian tutors." Asian Christians have taught him the importance of praying without ceasing and of reclaiming a missionary zeal. The strengths of Asian spirituality can be a real asset to the post-Christian church of the one-third world if the church is willing to listen and to learn. Mission is receiving as well as giving.

Bonnie Sue Lewis, of Dubuque Seminary, shares what she has learned about mission in working with Guatemalans and Native Americans. She has found that mission is primarily about listening. Because it is God's mission, we must first learn to listen to God. Then we must learn to listen to the deep cries of others, to be hospitable and welcome friendships and to allow for the witness of God's compassionate love. Lewis has learned to listen from those in the Guatemalan and Native American communities with whom she has partnered in mission.

Darrell Guder of Columbia Seminary wraps up these narratives with his focus on the congregation as a mission community sent to witness to the healing news of God's love. From his years of mission work in a post-Christendom Europe, he sees growing evangelizing congregations as God's strategy for mission. Therefore, seminaries must be about the business of forming pastors to be evangelists and missionaries.

These narratives gathered from the professors of mission in the Presbyterian seminaries illustrate that God is indeed doing a new thing in mission and in seminary education. We are encouraged by what we have found. There is a growing awareness of the scope and depth of God's mission in the world. There is also the recognition that God has raised up Christians worldwide to help bring in the harvest. Mission today means working with and learning from those with whom we serve. There is a new humility among those in mission that we believe touches God's heart and will allow God to fulfill his mission in the world. We believe that the faith journeys recorded here that inform the way mission is being taught in today's Presbyterian seminaries will also serve as a teaching tool for the church at large. May we have ears to hear what God is saying to the churches and feet willing to take us there.

Feet First

How Practices Have Shaped My Theology of Evangelism and Mission

FRANCES S. ADENEY

*N*ot long ago in the historic town of New Harmony, Indiana, I had the chance to walk through a labyrinth formed with tall green hedgerows. Although I knew I was progressing through the maze, at times it seemed as if I was retracing my steps, treading on familiar ground. This experience reminded me of practices in my own life that have occurred over and over, yet have reformed their meanings as I acted them out in new contexts at different stages of life while facing unique challenges. When one is walking a labyrinth, there are no vistas, no points on the horizon from which to judge one's location, no straight road ahead by which to gauge the remaining distance. One finds oneself looking frequently at one's feet.

I propose that we can find out much about what we believe by looking down at our feet: Where are they standing? Where have they roamed recently? Where are they headed? Our recurring patterns of living tell us about where we have been, where we are going, and what we believe about God, about other people, and about our world.[1]

Right now my feet are standing in a place called Louisville Seminary. My task here is to assess the situation for evangelism and mission for congregations in North America and to train pastors to develop theologies of mission that suit those contexts and are true to the Christian faith. As I develop this work, I look down at my feet. How did I get here? What practices shaped my thinking and action to bring me to this place, to this task? What do those practices mean for how I teach, do research, and formulate missiological theology and method? I refer to things we do routinely that, while seeming ordinary enough, inform our values and thinking and give shape to our lives—theological shape. What we do, even more than what we think we believe, shapes our theology.[2]

As I reflect on the labyrinth of my own life, I think of four central practices that have been with me for most of my adult years. Practices of silence, protest, community, and conversation have shaped my life. In various contexts and communities, I have revised these practices over the years. Each of them has influenced my coming to Louisville Seminary to study and teach evangelism and mission.

These practices did not initially spring from a clear theological mandate. They were formed in various ways: by family and community influence, by a desire to bring good into the world, by the longing for meaning and relationship. But as I reflected upon those practices, I began to understand my life differently. Reflecting on my actions and seeking to articulate the meaning of those practices yielded theologies. I became more intentional about what I believed as I followed my feet and thought about the intentional actions in my life. As those theologies became articulate, a praxis developed that joined thought and action together. That new praxis led to further reflection and reconsideration, both of what I believed and of the practices themselves. That thoughtful reflection led to new thinking and subsequently changed my practices. The result of this process became a revised praxis.[3]

This process of practice/reflection/theology/praxis did not occur in a linear fashion, although it must be described in that way. Sometimes a theological insight pressed me into immediate action. At other times, theological understanding lagged behind my actions. Overall, an overlapping, spiraling circle of interpretation characterized the process.

Following my feet, engaging in theological analysis of my life and actions with communities of faith, and revising both theology and actions in light of the effects of those practices, took me through a rich labyrinth of missionary service and academic study that brought me to focus on missiology as a profession and a calling. I speak about this process narratively, which is how my theology has been formed.[4] Let me tell you something about how silence, protest, community, and conversation have shaped my life.

Silence

Sunlight caught the wineglass and it burst out red as the old man lifted off the white cloth. From my vantage point under the grand piano, the cloth seemed almost to be floating above the table. The old hands folded it delicately, slowly, as if time didn't matter. Finally, he intoned the familiar words, "On the night that he was betrayed, Jesus took bread, and when he had given thanks, he broke it, saying, 'This is my body which is broken for you. Do this in remembrance of me.'"[5]

I was three years old when my parents, both from Catholic families, began attending a Plymouth Brethren assembly in Summerville, New Jersey. The "meeting" was held in a house up a dirt lane across the highway. The Harold Crane family and a few others gathered from 11:00 to 12:00 every Sunday in the Crane living room, forming a circle around a small mahogany table upon which was set a loaf of Mrs. Crane's fresh bread and a crystal decanter of dark red wine. Those elements remained covered with a white cloth until almost precisely 11:50, at which time Mr. Crane or Mr. Ross, the only two men considered old enough to have the privilege, would solemnly rise, walk to the center of the room, and preside over the symbolic feast.[6]

Most of that hour was spent in silence—serious silence, communal silence, sacred silence. It was the first Christian practice in which I participated. Even when I sat with a coloring book under the grand piano, I knew that this place, this hour, these spare and singular acts, were wonderfully special. Those worship meetings influenced my personality, shaped my faith, and brought me into sacred time—a sacred time that I continue to seek out wherever I am.

Through participating in an hour of communal silence nearly every Sunday from 1947 to 1974, silence became my first practice. I attended "meeting" in Plymouth Brethren assemblies in Summerville; Oak Park, Illinois; Friendship, Wisconsin; Anoka, Minnesota; London, England; and Singapore. Once, on a visit to France in 1970, I found a Brethren meeting, and was amazed to hear identical hymn tunes, feel the familiar solemnity, and see the same ritual performed in a culture and language that were strange to me.

The theology that grew from these experiences affirmed the unity of the body of Christ, the cross-cultural relevance of the Christian faith, and the importance of Sabbath rest and worship. It also taught me something about God—something about the awe that God inspires by God's Presence, something about the presence of the Holy Spirit and the communion of saints, something about the "beatific vision."[7] For it was that which we saw somehow—together—without words.

Understanding awe as the universal response of the whole church before God now aids me in thinking about the mission of the church in the twenty-first century.[8] This tremendous experience, fostered in my life by communal silence, happens in other ways too. Such awe before God's Presence is relevant anywhere, anytime, in any culture. And it happens, not only in personal worship or when churches foster it, but whenever searching people gather around the Word or sacraments. God graciously gives the experience of awe to seekers of truth, alone or together, with or without "correct" theological understandings.

While good theology is necessary to evangelism, the apostle Paul made it clear that even when the gospel was preached out of a spirit of partisanship or for personal gain, he rejoiced that the gospel was preached at all (Phil. 1:15–18; 1 Tim. 6:5). Whether speaking out of rivalry and envy or out of goodwill, those preachers would not "convert" people or even inspire change in their lives. But God, through that preaching, might give people an experience of Presence that would bring them to faith. And that is all that mattered.

In 1974, with my husband and two little girls, I moved to Berkeley, California, where I participated in house church worship that had moments of silence but was much more lively, active, and verbal. I still experienced the awe of Presence in worship, but silence as a spiritual discipline was lost to me for some years.

The practice of entering silence was revived as a personal form of prayer in 1993 as I was living in Indonesia as a Presbyterian mission coworker. Culture shock, combined with the death of my father and a chronic bronchial condition, motivated me to seek a connection with God that could nurture my inner spirit. Cut off from so many of the normal cues that led me to worship, I learned to practice silence, to enter silence as a form of prayer. That practice sustained me through the years in Indonesia, years of loss as well as adventure. The theology of awe spread for me from the communal to the personal arena, and I continue to be nurtured by it.

Surprising as it may seem, learning to practice silence as a personal spiritual discipline taught me something about ecumenical dialogue as well. My physical condition required rest, which I found at Gedono, a Trappist monastery for women on the mountain near my home in Salatiga. The Catholic sisters welcomed me, and provided quiet space and time for me to seek out God again. Later I received spiritual direction from a Jesuit priest in Salatiga who helped me explore a world of self-understanding and personal spirituality that I hadn't known existed.

In Indonesia, the Catholic and Protestant churches are considered two different religions. Suspicion and distance characterize relations between these groups of God's people. My experience with the Trappist sisters fostered communication between the monastery and the university and led to more Protestant visitors finding their way up the mountain for retreat. The practice of dialogue between Protestant and Catholic Christians, so common in the United States, is still difficult, not only in Indonesia, but in other parts of the world. Modeling the unity of the body of Christ through such effort is a crucial part of the mission of the church in the world.

Modeling such unity can be augmented by interreligious dialogue. Again, practices led the way to my understanding of the respect and love that we as Christians can exhibit toward those of other faiths. The contemplative prayer that Father Hamma showed me is not unlike the Buddhist practice of meditative silence. Through learning to enter silence in personal devotions, I gained an appreciation for Buddhist forms of worship.[9]

Protest

While it seemed to lead to quietism for some, encountering God in contemplative worship spurred me to action. I wanted to study, to travel, to understand God's world and how Christianity mattered. Mission biographies and devotional Christian readings augmented the serious study of the Bible encouraged by my Brethren assembly. I wanted to act.

No one predicted the form that zeal would take when I left my sheltered family life and went to the University of Wisconsin at Madison during the 1960s. The civil rights movement jolted me, expanding my world in agonizing ways. Seeing newsreels of police beating civil rights workers combined with my realizing the preposterous truth that some citizens in this country were threatened when they went to the polls. Violent images burned themselves into my mind—children slaughtered at My Lai, peaceful civil rights demonstrators attacked by National Guardsmen, antiwar protesters teargassed and herded into trucks. I joined protests against the war in Vietnam. Once during a prayer meeting on campus I looked out the window and saw police cars drive straight into crowds of protesters on the fountain mall at the university. I felt helpless while watching televised scenes from the war and reports of the assassinations of Martin Luther King and John F. Kennedy, and of the four Kent State University students who were killed by police during a peaceful demonstration. I didn't have to think much—the evils of the times came into my dorm room and I took to the streets.

Justice—on a large scale—occupied my outlook when I went to Berkeley in 1974 to work with the Christian World Liberation Front. A small but energetic group of hippies, we set up a drop-in house for the homeless, organized a "free university" where we taught Christian social ethics, and put out a journal on cults and new religious movements. From there I worked with Ron Sider's Discipleship Workshops, educating churches about the economics of international corporations. I demonstrated with Pacific Life Community against proliferation of nuclear arms. In the 1980s, I became concerned about U.S. involvement in Nicaragua, and in 1985 I traveled to the war-torn northern part of that country as part of a National Women's Delegation. Here I witnessed the patriotism of women who, though angered by their country's policies in Central America, cared enough to endanger their lives communicating their loyal opposition to the nation.[10] Two bullets whizzed past my own ears one day while working in the field. After a windy march along the northern border where the women planted crosses at the site of slain soldiers and civilians, I arrived back in the United States with a sliver of metal embedded in my left eye that nearly cost me my sight.[11]

Action characterized these years in other ways too. Raising three children, copastoring a house church, and earning my Ph.D. kept me focused and involved in spiritual and intellectual communities. But justice occupied my mind and protest took my feet to fascinating, sometimes frightening places.

As I reflect on the theology of mission that grew out of that period in my life, a number of themes stand out. First, the practice of protest for me sprang out of a conviction that justice should "roll down like waters, righteousness like a mighty stream" (Amos 5:24). Studying liberation theologies at the Graduate Theological Union in the mid-1980s only confirmed what my heart and my society already knew—that oppression is wrong, that liberation is right, that justice is the will of God.[12] The theology is one of hope—hope that change can happen despite human evil, hope that, although unseen, God is at work in the world.[13] That hope cannot but result in action, and leads, for me, into a theology of participation with God's actions of love and justice in the world.

That participation is also tied to a love for democracy and a sense of responsibility to participate in the affairs of my nation.[14] I protested as a citizen, loyal to my country while dissenting from particular policies of the government. I learned to stand up for a cause, rejecting the complacency that can arise from a sense of inability to affect the political process in our huge nation.[15] I have carried that political concern with me into my study of missions. Christianity is not a private religion based solely on individual feelings and relegated to home life and church services. God's acts through the people of God are public and seek to influence for good all of the spheres of life on earth: social and political as well as personal and religious.

Community

The energy for social protest and the concerted action it requires spring from community. Not only the communities that formed within the antiwar movement but also the communities that sustained the Christian feminist movement and the antinuclear protests were crucial to my life of faith during the 1970s. Centered in practices of dialogue and public action, they fostered the development of my theology of justice and equality as well as my present-focused theology of God's action in the world through God's people.

But much more than protest happens in communities. Mutual support, outreach in ministry, learning and interpreting the faith together, and the joy of worship are some of the benefits of Christian community. In Madison during the late 1960s, I was centered in the InterVarsity Christian community. Later in Berkeley, as well as earlier in Singapore, I lived in intentional Christian communities. Life in those communities shaped my view of how God works in the world.[16]

My first lessons of community were commitment and hospitality. As one of eight children, I learned early in life to value sharing and to take up my responsibilities in the family. While loyalty to the family was stressed, welcoming others seemed equally important. Guests were always welcome in our home despite economic hardship, and, by bringing up jars of canned vegetables and fruit from the cellar, somehow there was always enough. Like the Muslim neighbors I later grew to love in Indonesia, our family believed that welcoming the stranger was part of our duty. As children we often heard the story of Abraham and Sarah who "entertained angels unaware" as my father liked to phrase it. We too needed to be ready to welcome those who needed hospitality from us. Once my mother gave a plate of food to a beggar who had come to our door. Although I was only five, I was pretty sure he wasn't an angel. But my mother gave him food anyway.

Later, living in a Christian study community in Singapore, I learned to sustain commitment to a community through the difficulties of *being* that stranger. As one of two students from the West, I learned to eat rice twice a day and work with people from ten different Asian countries. The tropical heat stultified my husband and me during the hour-long bus ride out to the Brethren assembly with our first, sometimes fussy, baby in tow. The daily round of dried fish or okra with rice became increasingly difficult to enjoy, and the strenuous study program of Greek, Isaiah, New Testament, and theology, along with the inevitable tensions among students from different cultures, combined to frustrate efforts to learn well and live in harmony. I was required to call upon that commitment that I had learned as a child—to persevere with those God had put in my life and to offer hospitality in any way I could. I needed those commitments to stay the course.

Later, in our Christian community in Berkeley, I found that that same sense of commitment to others brought tremendous rewards as we shared life together. Our Bible study group decided on the community venture, bought a house together, renovated it, and established it as The Ark, a place that, though full of an assortment of odd people, was a refuge. My three children had "aunts" and "uncles" aplenty to play games, listen to their woes, take them on outings, and generally teach them that extended family was the only way to go. We learned to work, play, argue, support one another, laugh together, and finally to say goodbye. When this community disbanded in 1985, we found our ways into churches as diverse as the Friends, Roman Catholic, Russian Orthodox, Covenant, Episcopal, and Presbyterian. This experience showed me, in a way that goes beyond words, the unity of the body of Christ.

The practice of community living also taught me that perfection is not necessary to good living, that diversity is an asset and not a liability to group solidarity, and that the old Anabaptist notion of the church as a community of witness—a place that shows forth the kingdom by example—is not such a strange notion after all. Seeing the church both as Presence in the world and as source of support became a conscious theology for me. We were connected to the world, engaged in the issues of the day, and yet supported by a communion that nurtured us—and there was always enough.

Conversation

One of the most meaningful experiences in that community was our practice of discussing the meaning of life and its values. My children, who were subjected to those long dinner conversations, would lament, "Oh no, do we have to talk about ethics again?" While sometimes too long to engage the children's imaginations, those discussions were part of a serious practice of seeking to relate the teaching of the Bible and Christian tradition to our everyday lives.

I learned as a young person to study the Bible seriously and to spend a part of each day in conversation with God. I also learned to discuss questions of faith with others and to "converse" with the writings of theologians. Bible commentaries, works of theology, and historical biographies lined my bookshelves, propped up by the stuffed animals and jewelry boxes that suited my youthful fancy.

Another kind of conversation that I sought as a young person was rooted in my curiosity to understand the unfamiliar and get to know those who were different from me.[17] As a high school student, I dreamed about traveling to Europe. "Why?" one of my brothers asked in exasperation. "What can they possibly have in Europe that we don't have here?" Lots, to my mind. Eventually I got over there, and when I did I discovered Paris and Notre Dame, Switzerland and L'Abri Fellowship, Florence and Donatello, Austria and the Alps. Most interesting though were the people my husband and I met—a French man with whom we shared maps, pointing to places we had been, a young man with whom we traded only names of music groups (the Beatles; Crosby, Stills, Nash, and Young; Led Zeppelin), each punctuated by exclamations of pleasure and affirmation.

Other conversations had more substance. We spent the spring equinox one year at Stonehenge, talking all night with young Druids, processing with them around the stones, hearing what brought them into that religion, talking about what Christianity meant to us. Back in the United States, we started a coffeehouse at the University of Wisconsin, Madison. The idea was to create a contemporary atmosphere, offer some good coffees and teas, and stimulate discussion around the meaning of life. If the conversation turned to religious belief and the moment seemed right, we were ready to talk about Christian faith. If not, we figured that raising questions about the meaning of life was a valuable enterprise in itself.

Unwittingly, we were practicing the kind of reflexive evangelism that the apostle Paul demonstrates in Acts 17. Paul travels to Athens and, while anxious to talk to the Jews about Jesus, he listens to other religious voices, he learns the wisdom of their poets and philosophers, he makes a connection between their quest for the unknown God and the God of his message, and he speaks of the resurrection in the clearest possible terms. First, Paul takes the "way of the common," paying serious attention to the views of others and finding the common threads with his own understanding of God. Then he takes the "way of the strange," clearly articulating the death and resurrection of Jesus and explicating its meaning for humans.[18]

Besides a theology of evangelism that listens as well as speaks, that learns as well as teaches, the theology that grows out of these experiences is one of delight in diversity, respect and honor for others and their views, and enjoyment of cultural exchange. It is an approach to conversation about meaning that attends and listens first. Genuine interest in others and in their point of view, combined with the possibility that I too will be changed through the interaction, is at the heart of this process.[19]

Conversation was at the heart of my mission work when I went to Indonesia in 1991 as a Presbyterian mission coworker. The University of Satya Wacana in Java asked me to help develop a graduate program in religion and society. The goal of the program was to train Indonesian professors, church leaders, and pastors to understand and augment the public role of the church in Indonesia. The heart of this task was conversational. I needed to listen, first to the invitation by our partner church in Indonesia, then to the experience of church and society that they had. Next, I offered tools of analysis and theoretical insights into their situation, which I had to check out with them regarding their value in the Indonesian context. Only then could any offer of Western ideas, methods, or educational techniques become useful. And those ideas only proved useful as Indonesians modified them to fit their cultural situation. The entire enterprise was a conversation between partners.

The five years that I spent teaching in Indonesia solidified my view of mission as partnership. I see no place for a relationship with Christians of other countries in which Western theologies or methods take precedence.[20] Local theologies developed in context by people of different cultures are needed. Western voices can be heard as part of the chorus, but not as the solo voice. I found it incredibly rewarding to share my academic expertise with Indonesian teachers and learners while I learned from their insights into society and theology. The process modeled the partnership I believe we need as Christians from many countries interact with one another, reach out to the lost and needy, and put into action our unity in Christ.

My understanding of Christian faith and how my life fits into the Christian story is built upon a contextual understanding of the other and an appreciation for the beliefs and ways of the other. I find that when I listen, others want to hear my story too. And the story of the cross is an easy one to hear, despite its folly. On many a late night here in the United States, in Nicaragua, in the Philippines, in Pakistan, and in Indonesia, I heard stories of faith that moved me. Sometimes I told my story, the old story of God's love in Jesus—a story that shines like a jewel because it changes lives and because, I believe, it is true.

Conclusion

My theology has not been static over a lifetime but has changed as I have followed my feet and reflected upon where they have taken me.

I have been influenced by the communities of which I have been a part and have taken part in their traditions and activities, many of which have become part of my own practices. I have changed through the influence of mentors along the way, and through study, not only of scripture and books, but of films, art, and nature. I have been changed through the example and instruction of my children.

I have chosen pathways at many crossroads and sometimes those choices have led to difficulties as well as joys. Other paths, not consciously chosen, nevertheless found their way into my feet. But in every path, I have seen (sometimes afterwards) the providential care, the stern or loving hand, of God. I sense the presence of the Holy Spirit in my life and in the world.

The questions about evangelism and mission facing the church at the beginning of the twenty-first century are too complex to be answered by any one person. But as communities, we can both learn from and influence our context. As I take up the task of understanding and teaching evangelism and mission at Louisville Seminary, I will study and act, reflect and revise my views in the context of the seminary, the church, and the world in which I live. This praxis methodology is at the heart of both my learning and my teaching.

As this circle of meaning-making continues, I will be influenced by the practices I have developed in my unique life situations and concrete Christian communities. I will be nurtured and changed by the influences of those life practices that have developed in me a theology of awe of God, a sense of the unity of the church, an expectation of justice in the world, a commitment to growing in community, and a love for conversation about meaning and the gospel.

NOTES

1. Alasdair MacIntyre in *After Virtue* (Notre Dame, Ind.: University of Notre Dame Press, 1981) applies Aristotle's notion of habits to our modern Western milieu (chapter 12). In this view, character is formed, not by beliefs or convictions, but by daily repetition of acts that eventually become habitual, comprising the virtues that result in good character (140f.). I would argue further that practices not only mold our lives but inform our theology.

2. In his book *The Shape of Living: Spiritual Directions for Everyday Life* (Grand Rapids: Baker, 1998), David F. Ford speaks of the experience of being overwhelmed, and outlines a number of responses to that feeling that can be formed into daily practices of living, practices that acknowledge in concrete ways our human limitations and the awesomeness of God.

3. Liberation theologies—Latin American, black, and feminist/womanist/mujerista—emphasize this praxis methodology, linking didactic theologies to prac-

tice through bringing together real-life context and action with biblical texts and theological reflection. See Maria Harris, *Proclaim Jubilee: A Spirituality for the Twenty-First Century* (Louisville, Ky.: Westminster John Knox, 1996) for a good example of this methodology.

4. H. Richard Niebuhr spoke of revelation occurring in our lives and communities as we tie our own life story into the biblical account. Rather than a personalistic, purely experiential theology on the one hand, or a purely rationalistic theology on the other, Niebuhr argued that the revelation of God happens in communities of faith, resulting in confessional theologies that are linked to the Christian tradition while engaging contemporary life (*The Meaning of Revelation*, New York: Macmillan [1941], 1960, 44). This gives theology a narrative structure. It can be done "from below," from within our communities and life histories, growing out of ordinary life experience, while finding meaning and truth in relation to the patterns and meanings of the biblical narratives.

5. It was many years before I came to realize that these familiar words of institution from 1 Cor. 11:23–26f were used almost universally among Protestant and Catholic congregations in the Communion/Eucharist celebration.

6. The Grant-Kelly Plymouth Brethren grew out of the English Brethren movement begun in the mid-nineteenth century in England by J. N. Darby. This Anglican reform movement emphasized the unity of the church as expressed through the breaking of bread. While Darby insisted on welcoming to the Lord's Supper any believer who practiced Christian faith and morality, some groups later became "exclusive," arguing that only those belonging to the fellowship or recommended by a respected member could partake of the bread and wine during this meeting. The small Grant-Kelly Brethren group that my family joined was "exclusive" in this way.

7. Although this term is used most frequently in Catholic theology, John Calvin too emphasized the importance of the frequent use of the sacrament of communion, referring to it as "taking the sacred mystery" (*Institutes*, Book 4, chaps. 17, 44 and 45).

8. Charles Taylor suggests that modern Western people need to link personal resonances with philosophical or theological concepts, or possibly even an outside order, in order to find moral sources that have meaning for them. (For an explanation of this idea, see my review of Taylor's *Sources of the Self: The Making of the Modern Identity*, in *Theology Today* 48, no. 2, July 1991.) The experience of awe can provide a link to a Christian understanding of God's actions of grace and salvation through Jesus Christ.

9. I was prepared to learn this practice years before through a course taught by Father O'Hanlon at the Graduate Theological Union. Each class began with five minutes of silence, a time marked off by the sound made by striking a small pottery bowl with a covered mallet. The course was on the writings of Thomas Merton, who consistently linked contemplation with action for justice in the world.

10. See "Desert Blooms: Nicaraguan Women of the '80s" in *Radix Magazine* 16, no. 5 (March/April 1985), 18–21; and "Nicaragua: A U.S. Problem?" in *Update: Newsletter of the Evangelical Women's Caucus* 9, no. 3 (1985), 8–9.

11. Along with her big brother, I planted a cross next to a hole in the wall of an adobe house where a grenade had been tossed, killing a twelve-year-old girl asleep

in her bed. The sliver of metal that blew into my eye along the dusty country road probably had a military origin since machines were few in that region.

12. I find it curiously satisfying that a fountain in San Francisco dedicated to Martin Luther King attributes the prophet Amos's words, "Let justice roll down like waters," to King. King appealed not to a strange teaching but to that which the people of the United States already knew but had neglected to practice.

13. Martin Luther King's theology asserted that evil is a reality but that because it carries within itself the seeds of its own destruction, evil cannot permanently organize itself. The good, being more powerful and linked to God, will always triumph in the end. (See "The Death of Evil Upon the Seashore" in Martin Luther King Jr., *Strength to Love*, Philadelphia: Fortress Press, 1981, 77–82.) This theology posits an overarching view of God's power, thus giving reasons for the hope that "we shall overcome someday."

14. Early Catholic influences and my later study of Reformed theology convinced me that God is concerned with all of life and active in the affairs of the world, which we are called upon to manage as good stewards.

15. Michael Walzer in *Obligations* (Cambridge, Mass.: Harvard University Press, 1970, 216), argues that the size of our nation frustrates citizens who are taught to become involved in national affairs and feel responsible for them, yet have few institutionalized ways to effect change at the national level. Since then loyal protest, begun in the 1960s, has lodged itself in communities, developing a more sustained impact and acceptance as a legitimate form of political activity.

16. The idea that a pastor is in charge and responsible for a congregation, for example, is foreign to me. My community experiences and the theology of the laity that I learned in the Brethren emphasize the communal nature of Christian life and witness. While God raises up prophets, change comes about through communities of faith. The importance of each one fulfilling their responsibility in the larger community is crucial to this view.

17. I did not realize at the time that my own childhood experience was crosscultural. The Catholic culture of my extended family contrasted sharply with the Brethren social milieu that occupied so much of my early years. I have noticed among my students that the tensions engendered by such cross-cultural experiences in home life often lead to a desire to understand other cultures and religions.

18. The "way of the common" and the "way of the strange" are concepts that I learned from "The Importance of Not Understanding," an unpublished manuscript by Zaly Gurevitch, who teaches at Hebrew University, in Jerusalem. After participating in Palestinian-Jewish dialogue, he found that before real communication was possible, each side had to recognize that it did not understand the point of view of the other. A willingness to address this difference became the starting point for real dialogue.

19. Hans George Gadamer (*Truth and Method,* 2d rev. ed., New York: Continuum, 1996, 305–7) describes learning in this interpretive fashion. Learning begins with being open to the other by transposing oneself into the other's position. Encountering the other and interacting with him or her in this way expands one's horizon of meaning. I base my own hermeneutic circle on Gadamer's, adding an evaluative stage where openness to the other is balanced by an evaluative moment

that reconnects one to one's own tradition. See *Christians Encounter the World's Religions* by Frances Adeney (Grand Rapids: Baker, forthcoming).

20.   The postmodern turn has resulted in an understanding that all theology and philosophy is integrally connected to the location of a community—its perspective, history, and context. This understanding allows Asian voices to be heard in theology and requires humility on the part of Western theologians, who need to listen and learn to appreciate culturally different expressions of universal Christian faith.

PART II

Mission at the Margins

Mission at the Borders

*Developing Our Mission Theology
and Praxis through Biography and Testimony*

CARLOS F. CARDOZA-ORLANDI

In honor of my mentor and friend Alan Neely

We usually think about mission as the task of transmitting the gospel of Jesus Christ. We try to discover, develop, and implement the best possible theologies, strategies, and practices of mission in order to transmit the gospel with the best possible medium. We want people to listen to and to *understand* the good news of the reign of God. We do the best we can to make it accessible, understandable, and acceptable. Very few Christian congregations or missionaries will begin to preach the gospel by blunt confrontation or imposition. Even those considered "unsophisticated street preachers" in so many corners of our world usually begin their preaching with some connecting statement or idea that will capture the attention of their audience. Mission is about good, adequate transmission.

Many missiologists, Christian leaders, and congregations agree that there is a need to reassess our theologies and strategies (or lack thereof) of mission. I am convinced that many North American congregations want to be effective and successful in their missionary endeavors. Indeed, the purpose of this collection of essays is to contribute to the ongoing conversation about mission among Presbyterian congregations and in other mainline churches. I celebrate and participate in such an important task.

I want to propose, however, that the mission task needs to change focus from an emphasis on transmission to an emphasis on the contextualization of the gospel. Many times our exaggerated focus on transmission blinds our ability to "see" God's activity and wonders among people of other cultures and religions, many of whom are the focus of our transmission. Furthermore, our eagerness to "do" with efficiency and to successfully "complete" the missional project often makes us oblivious to the intriguing and fascinating dynamics of our encounters with people of other faiths and of different contexts, and of their relationship with the gospel in their rich and complex cultural, religious, and social reality.

Because transmission and partnership efforts are overwhelming in many congregations and denominations, those involved in missionary activity need to discover a symbolic/social place or location from where they can discern God's activity. From such a place they can not only think about the transmission of the gospel, but become aware that the reception of the gospel informs and shapes the way in which the people of God, both missionaries and missionized, receive and live the gospel in a particular context.

This symbolic/social location is a spiritual dwelling place. By spiritual I do not mean isolated from reality. On the contrary, this symbolic/social space is for discernment and discovery of God's wonders in our context and beyond. It is a location for repentance and contrition, for ethical and theological reflection, for prayer and meditation, and for reconciliation and celebration. It is a symbolic space because it does not have to be a particular space—such as a room or a chapel—but can be an inclination, an approach, a way of understanding and interpreting our faith in life and our life in faith.

This place is also a social space, because we are social beings. All we do and are shapes and is shaped by our ethnic background, our gender and sexual orientation, our age, our roles in family structures, our occupations, our salaries and our location in the social ladder, our congregational participation, and our understanding and practice of mission. Because it is a social space, on the one hand, we are unable to deceive ourselves, for if we try, other social groups will name who we are and will help us see and accept what we do not want to see and accept. For instance, I cannot claim to be a poor person in this world. My social location reminds me of my middle-class status in the context of the United States.

On the other hand, my social location can play games on me and may blur my self-understanding. For example, I have done mission in many places in the Caribbean, most of them impoverished. I remember coming back home and sharing with my congregation how grateful I was for the gifts God had given my family and me. In a very subtle way, I was giving thanks for not being poor, not being like those with whom I shared the gospel. Moreover, my congregation agreed with my declaration: many of them found themselves joining me in thanksgiving. Ironically, my social space and the congregation's social space provided me the opportunity to engage in mission. At the same time, the congregation's social space, in affinity with mine, obscured the distant but real connection between their poverty and my (our) wealth.

The lack of a spiritual dimension in this particular space prevented me and my congregation from wrestling with the difficult and ironic experience of being grateful to God for our well-being and becoming aware of our role in the economic injustices of the Caribbean region. This difficult, dual identity needs to be resolved with Christian integrity. Regretfully, our congregational structures of mission, as I mentioned above, do not provide the symbolic/social space to discern and come to terms with these complexities. Consequently, I want to suggest that the symbolic/social space to engage in missiological reflection is *the border.*

The border is the space between spaces. It is also the place of encounters. It is the place of mission.[1] It provides a space to gain perspective and insight. It helps accentuate the paradoxes, the conflicts, the dualism, and the false dichotomies that impede sound mission theologies and practices. This is the space where I want to invite the reader to think about the nature of mission. This article is, in a particular way, my missiological reflection at the borders. I have placed myself in a symbolic/social space where my biography, theology, and missiology find each other. But how will I articulate such an encounter? How will I communicate my reflection?

Biography as a Source
of Theology/Missiology: A Testimony

Rubem Alves describes the relationship between history, biography, and human interconnectedness in the following way:

> Biography and history go together. . . . The fact remains that our personal destiny is rooted deeply in the destiny of civilizations. In one way or another, our biography is always a symptom of the conditions prevailing in the world. That is the reason behind the discovery we all frequently make. Despite the fact that we live in different places, posts, and political contexts, our biographies strongly resemble slight variations of one and the same script. They have the same structures. They go through the same sequence of hopes and frustrations.[2]

In theater there is one script but many dramas. The script is the story of life; the dramas are the multiple ways in which human beings respond to the lows and highs. Some of us respond by fascination and excitement, while others are disinterested or skeptical. The sequence of hopes and frustrations, of certainties and ambiguities, of faith and doubt are responses that characterize human existence and creation. They illustrate the complex but common human dilemma of life.

For Alves, as stated above, this common human dilemma defines the connecting link between biography and history. But he goes further and proposes that the task of facing this common human dilemma with courage, sense of direction and meaning is the link between biography and theology:

> Theology and biography go together. . . . Religion is the proclamation of the axiological priority of the heart over the raw facts of reality. It is a refusal to be gobbled up and digested by the surrounding world, an appeal to a vision, a passion, a love.[3]

This "refusal to be gobbled up and digested by the surrounding world" shapes and informs our urgency for mission. On the other hand, this "appeal to a vision, a passion, a love," informs the complex interaction between gospel and cultures. In other words, the refusal to be dominated by the frustrations of this world and the appropriation of hope despite those frustrations is what informs the way in which the people (their vision, their passion, their love) appropriate the gospel and the way the gospel (the vision, the passion, and the love of God in Jesus Christ and through the Holy Spirit) appropriates the people. In missional jargon, this is the contextualization of the gospel and the "gospelization" of the context: transmission and reception become one reality.

Biography and theology find a medium of transmission and reception in testimony. In testimony, a community theologizes its biography and "biographs" its theology, ultimately shaping its missiology, its sense of being and doing through God in the world. In the Pentecostal tradition of my grandparents, testimony has a crucial role in defining the character of the faith of a believer and a community. Testimony is the speech and act that integrates the gospel story with the believer's and the community's stories. Testimony has levels of maturity. The speech and act achieves higher levels of maturity as (1) the gospel story moves from an individual story to a communal story and (2) the speech and act shifts or emphasizes the "act" dimension of testimony. It is this last principle that makes the connection with mission. Ultimately, mission is not only about telling the story of the gospel or my story of the gospel, but rather communicating to the broader community in speech and act the story of the gospel intertwined with the story of the broader community. It is communal journaling of God's activity in the community! Therefore, mission is the sharing of our testimony, of our biography, of our struggle to see, hear, smell, touch, and taste God's performance in the drama of our lives in creation's common script.

As contextualized Christians, we can only refer to our own experiences as we reflect on our testimonies. For instance, ask yourself the following questions: Can you name any person in your extended family whose faith is non-Christian? Can you identify within your family any radical social class differences? Can you identify within your family radical ideological differences—not the traditional, predominant conservative/liberal categories of the United States, but radically different positions such as laissez-faire capitalism and socialism? I have met very few people in the United States who can answer any of these questions in the affirmative.[4] The family members of most Christians are also Christian, or at least claim sympathy with Christianity, and most belong to the same social class, and most have a common core of beliefs that shape and support the present political system and government structure. It seems that family history is reasonably steady and consistent, especially if some of the "unfortunate mixing" of family members is well hidden. (I believe that some of those hidden stories hold a reservoir of growth that we cannot realize unless they are uncovered.)

Most third world Christians, however, find themselves answering these questions with a resounding Yes! Christians in the third world work, eat, and relate on a daily basis with people of other faiths, of different ethnic backgrounds, of different social classes, of different ideologies. Moreover, congregations are grappling, intentionally or unintentionally, with the meaning of the gospel of Jesus Christ as it interacts with their diverse cultures. They are constantly found at the borders.

The interaction of the Christian faith with other historical, cultural, social, and political realities in the third world is due to the communal character of life in those countries. The life of faith is not isolated from the dynamics of daily life, though one's multiple religious, cultural, and social experiences may be different from the Christian faith. Faith is in constant interaction, penetrating and being penetrated by daily *praxis*.[5] Thus, the vitality of Christianity in the third world is due to the interaction of faith with the multiple factors of life. Faith and life are intrinsically related.

We could ask: Is the faith in the West not related to diverse factors in daily life as well? Certainly it is. However, the relationship is not the same. On the one hand, as I have already indicated, the Christian faith in the West tends to assume its own context to be either Christian or secular-capitalist—the latter a context traditionally considered an ally of the faith in some circles, or at least an enemy whose benefits can be enjoyed.

Frequently the Christian faith finds itself either completely tied to culture or claiming to be totally removed from culture.[6] This cultural dynamic does not permit a critical interaction in which the gospel modifies daily life and daily life *modifies the gospel*.[7]

On the other hand, the profoundly individualistic and compartmentalized nature of the dominant culture in North America presumes an autonomy and independence that obstructs the possibility of cultural and religious interaction and interpenetration. This nature found grounding in philosophers such as Johann Gottlob Herder who "put forward the idea that each of us has an original way of being human: each person has his or her own 'measure.'" Consequently, there is a particular way of being human—my way! This idea has become entrenched in modern Western consciousness, an ideology of human identity in isolation. Such a proposition, as difficult as it is for North American Christians to admit, is culturally unquestionable.[8]

All human identities and communities are dialogical in nature. This insight is what I affirm third world missiology can contribute to North American missiology. Given our ideology of identity in isolation, the question we face is: Can human beings achieve a sense of identity in an individual and monological inward way? Charles Taylor, the Canadian philosopher answers,

> in the nature of the case, there is no such thing as inward generation, monologically understood. In order to understand the close connection between identity and recognition, we have to take into account a crucial feature of the human condition that has been rendered almost invisible by the overwhelming monological mainstream modern philosophy. . . . This crucial feature of human life is its fundamental dialogical character.[9]

The above assumes that the Christian faith, together with multiple cultural, social, and political realities, has the capacity to form the personal and communal biography of the people of God. For example, the struggle for daily bread or the challenge of interacting daily with neighbors who profess another faith creates a unique relational dynamic[10] that generates reflection on the faith that goes further than the traditional parameters of Western theological reflection (e.g., the Bible, tradition, denominational polity). Here I want to emphasize that I am not referring to experience as a criterion for theological reflection (much has been said about this) but rather to the interaction between faith and life, the mutual penetration of realities that can only be discerned from the borders.

Testimonies and Mission

In my reflection from the borders I have come to the conclusion that the resources for mission theologies and practices are varied and at times in contradiction to each other. In my personal life, however, born in what I was told was an evangelical household, I was kept at a distance from other religious sources and cultural practices considered a threat to my evangelical identity. I was kept on one side of the border, secure and protected. I was never allowed to walk to the *border* or even to cross it, unless it was for the purpose of evangelism or simply because I did not have any other choice.

Ironically, it was not until I began my education at Princeton and was forced to take on an ethnic identity—Hispanic/Latino (hence, placed at a border)—that I began to discover new sources for mission theology and practices. First, I become aware that my way of being a global Protestant Christian is not the only one; rather, the way I understand and live the gospel is particular to my historical and cultural context. I am reminded of one crucial lesson taught by my mentor and friend Alan Neely at Princeton Seminary:

> Two conditions [for the communication of the gospel] appear undeniable and inescapable. First, the gospel is not nor can it be a-historical. If it is to be understood and appropriated, it will have to be rooted in a particular historical context. But as the gospel is never a-historical, neither can it be *a-cultural.* Christians assert that Jesus was a historical person, and being historical, Jesus was chronologically, geographically, religiously, and culturally a first-century Jew. He neither repudiated his humanity nor his Jewishness.[11]

Consequently, I have learned *that missiology and Christian identity are mutually shaped and dependent: my Christian identity informs my mission imperative just as my mission theology and practice is a prism of my Christian identity.*

As I mentioned above, I was raised in an evangelical household. My mother's family can trace its Methodist background to the first converts by North American missionaries. My great-granduncle was one of the first Puerto Ricans to be ordained in the Methodist Church in Puerto Rico. North American missionaries cared for my grandmother while her mother worked many hours during the day. At home, my evangelical identity was defined over and against Roman Catholicism.

On my father's side, however, the story was different, though never talked about. It is evident that in his family story the boundaries between

Protestantism and Roman Catholicism are blurred. I remember looking in my grandmother's and grandaunt's closets and finding necklaces made of beads with a cross attached to them. I also remember my parents' explanation of such artifacts: "Your grandaunt is a business woman, she sells and buys many things." It was not until I was assigned to a Disciples congregation in a remote, strongly Roman Catholic rural community that I learned that those necklaces were rosaries and that my father's family, though some were members of the Presbyterian Church in Puerto Rico, continued to say the rosary and attend mass from time to time.

During a recent Holy Week, I preached at the Presbyterian church where my father is an ordained elder and the treasurer of the congregation. In my Good Friday sermon, I referred to the suffering of Jesus at the cross as a witness of God's solidarity with those in suffering and pain. That evening my father asked me, "Why is it wrong to have a crucifix? Is not the crucifix a symbol of God's love for all of us? Why is it that we evangelicals have dismissed the crucifix? I do not think it is a bad symbol." I had to hold myself to the chair as I heard my father's statements. Was my father giving himself—and therefore me—permission to appropriate a symbol that has been identified with superstition and idolatry by missionaries and the early generation of Puerto Rican Protestants?[12]

Of all the members of my family, those who are Roman Catholic are the poorest, yet the strongest in times of daily adversity. They have always demonstrated tenacity and incredible persistence to keep themselves alive. They have also been the most ecumenical in the practice of their faith. I can remember when my parents visited them at the other side of the island and would ask them to join in prayer, in their own home, to ask for God's help. I never witnessed disrespect or apprehension when my parents prayed. I have to wonder what would have been the reaction of my parents if my Roman Catholic relatives would have offered a rosary or a prayer to the Virgin for our well-being.

This raises the question of mission to nominal Christians. Should we evangelize and do mission among the nominal Christians? The question I raise as I reflect upon this critical issue is this: How do we conclude that those to be evangelized and missionized are nominal Christians? How much Christian witness have my Roman Catholic relatives given to their community despite the fact that we consider them "nominal"? As a result, *sound mission theology and practice cannot be monolithic or rigid; it needs to be open to the wind of the Spirit as we are guided beyond the mission categories that define who should or should not be evangelized/ missionized.*

My third pastorate in Puerto Rico was in the coastal town of Dorado, in the barrio of Santa Rosa. Dorado is one of the towns in Puerto Rico with a high percentage of people of African descent. I was a pastor of a congregation of mostly African Puerto Ricans and a number of people with mixed ethnic/racial backgrounds. It was one of my most exciting pastorates on the island.

One evening I received a phone call from a woman named Juanita. Juanita was a leader of the Roman Catholic parish in the adjacent barrio. She had asked one of the members of my congregation for my phone number. She urgently needed to see me and talk to me. I agreed to come to her home.

Juanita was around fifty years old when I met her and her husband for the first time. She seemed very quiet and reserved, even fragile. I asked what I could do for her. She stared at me for some time. I began to feel uncomfortable and asked again, "Juanita, what can the church of Santa Rosa and I do for you?"

Juanita gave me a big smile. She said, "Pastor, I am dying. I have terminal cancer and I know I will not live for long. But I am well." I was saddened by her words. But there was some kind of certainty about what was going on in her life that amazed me. Then she asked, staring at me as she had done before, "Pastor, do you believe in spirits?"

That was it! Juanita was one of the mediums, one of the spirit-mediators, in the community. How could I have forgotten when I had heard so many stories of her kindness and care for so many people, including some of the members of my congregation who consulted her in secret? I wondered, What does this woman need from me?

We spent two hours talking to each other. Yes, we talked about spirits. She even suggested that I be more sympathetic to the world of the spirits. She said, "Pastor, you can find them in the Bible and not all of them are bad spirits." She talked about the "gift" she had received from God to help so many people. She lamented that her children had not received the gift, though they heard mass and had the Eucharist every Sunday. Juanita seemed to be happy with her life, but she had a heavy heart and a deep concern for many disoriented people in the barrio. She asked me, "Pastor, will you help them?" Can I help spiritists? I thought. Just before I left, Juanita asked me if I would pray for her. She asked her husband to bring the Bible. She gave it to me and said, "Read, Pastor, read your favorite psalm." We read and prayed . . . together!

The encounter with people of primal religious traditions continues to be a difficult but critical topic among missiologists. The work by the African theologian Kwame Bediako and the Scottish historian Andrew Walls, among others, has begun to open a path in missiological circles.[13] Consequently, *theologies and practices of mission need to address with courage and integrity the difficult issues of Christianity's encounter with popular religions and religiosity. Theologies and mission practices for the twenty-first century cannot disregard these religious experiences and their social reality as superstitious, subcultural, marginal, or demonic without a thorough engagement and theological sensibility.*

Puerto Ricans and other people from the Caribbean both celebrate and deny our African heritage.[14] We celebrate it when it points to our music, our sense of rhythm, our ability to cope in difficult situations, and our beauty and sexuality. We deny it when it points to economic and social status, to our religious worldview, and to interracial and interethnic marriages. In a course I taught in Jamaica, one of my students from the island nation of Montserrat commented that she never had a problem with the dreadlocks of Rastafarian groups until her daughter began to grow them during a period of searching for her Caribbean identity. The Afro-Caribbean heritage is a "double edge" reality to many of us.

This condition of acceptance and denial of a particular cultural or religious trait is not exclusively Caribbean. Christian and non-Christian people and communities find themselves in this constant religious traffic and negotiation: it is characteristic of the hybrid postmodern identity and it should be an interesting issue in missiological circles.

At another time in my life I was a pastor in a Disciples congregation on the West Side of Manhattan in New York City. I served a congregation in which most members were from the Dominican Republic. A young family had recently visited the congregation. They became very excited about "how we are church," and became members.

The oldest boy in this young family became very sick. Our congregation developed prayer chains and held vigils for the child and the family. The child's health, however, worsened. The family stopped attending worship for a month or so. When they returned they had a healthy boy and joy in their spirits. After some time, some of the elders of the congregation asked me if I could visit the family to find out if certain rumors about their faith were true. The elders indicated that this family practiced Santería and that they needed to be "disciplined" by the congregation. They told me that they discovered this after the child's health had improved.

I did visit the family, knowing that this was going to be a very difficult conversation. I did not have the slightest idea of how to bring up the rumors. Should I simply confront the family with the rumors? Should I introduce the issue by using a biblical example or some sort of communication strategy? The conversation began pleasantly. But I had to raise the issue.

I told the father that I had heard some rumors from the community regarding some Santería practices that were not congruent with our faith. I also expressed my concern for the well-being of the family and the good intentions of the congregation in exploring these rumors. I noticed that the father was upset, the mother had left the room, and the atmosphere was tense.

The father said that they had gone to a *babalawo* to seek advice and health. He said that he had no money to spend on doctors "who could not cure his son." He also said that he was grateful for the care and the prayers that the congregation had offered to God. But his son was in need, and he had to do something. He said that he visited the *babalawo* and followed the instructions for applying ointments and herbals to the boy's body. He also said that the *babalawo* insisted that a doctor should check the child and that the church's prayers were important.

In a sudden change of attitude, the father asked me what he had done wrong. I did not have an immediate answer to his concern, but a question slipped through my lips: "Brother, who do you think is the author of the healing of your son?" The father looked at me with astonishment and replied, "Christ, pastor, Christ. You are the theologian, you should know this better than I."

Christian theologies and practices of mission need to develop a stronger missiological base to recognize and critically engage the continuous religious traffic and negotiations in the life of many in our communities and congregations, particularly among the marginalized and the poor. The missiological issue is syncretism and justice. However, the history and use of the term *syncretism*—especially in theological circles—dismisses the complexity of the encounter and the possible avenues to face this common and very usual practice in the life of communities. Furthermore, issues of immigration, poverty, and injustice are usually ignored when studied side by side with issues of ethnicity and religious practices, resulting in fragmentation of the life of persons and communities.

My teaching at Columbia Theological Seminary has been exciting, though not without challenges. As the professor of world Christianity, I have taken the responsibility of offering courses that will help students understand the religious context where Christianity has vitality. Some of these courses focus on world religions, but with a particular emphasis on the encounter of these faiths with different traditions of Christianity.

One popular course among my electives is "World Religions and the Encounter with the Global Church." A critical component of this course is our visits to different religious communities. The visits are carefully planned and organized. I take time to prepare the students and provide them with some guidelines for proper conduct when we visit the sacred places. I try to be thorough and comprehensive in this area.

Among our visits is the Ismaili Jamatkhana (Center) of Decatur. The Ismaili tradition (Islam) has the characteristic of not allowing visitors to enter the place of worship, the hall of prayer. I tell my students that we will be warmly welcomed and that we will have a tour of the facilities of the Jamatkhana. I also tell them about the restrictions regarding the place of prayer and worship. On one such visit, one of my colleagues and his students joined us, despite having had no preparation for the visit.

As the tour came to an end, we faced the beautiful doors of the prayer hall, which were closed. Suddenly, the president of the Jamatkhana asked for the doors to be opened and invited us to remove our shoes and enter the prayer hall. The reaction of the students was astonishing. My colleague and his group rushed to take their shoes off and entered with no hesitation. I was frozen. I could not move or say anything. My students looked at me, waiting for some sort of indication. I looked at the president and he just smiled. We entered with apprehension, and yet with awe. I finally understood Rudolf Otto's *mysterium tremendum.* It was as if we had compelled our Muslim friends to partake of the Eucharist!

These visits have another interesting side. I have been invited by some friends of other faiths to teach in their religious schools about Christianity, Caribbean religiosity, and culture. On a particular occasion I was invited to teach at the Vedanta Center of Atlanta. My friend Swami Yogeshananda had extended me an invitation to speak about Afro-Caribbean religions and the Christian faith. As I was concluding my remarks, I shared with the congregation the results of a survey that revealed two important reasons why people converted to Christianity from the Afro-Caribbean religions. The first reason was that people were liberated from the fear that overwhelmed their relationship with the spirits. The second was that people were able to live in community and to trust others. I never thought I would get the response I got from most of the members of the Vedanta Center: "You have just revealed the reasons why we left our Christian churches!" Could this be an explanation for the crisis of the North American mainline churches?

The challenge and mystery of the Christian encounter with people of other faiths can be described further with the following testimony. Our oldest son was invited to spend the night at the home of one of his Jewish friends. His friend's father asked him if he wanted to participate in the evening prayers during Hanukkah. Carlos Andrés asked if he could have some time to think about it. He told us that he first thought about what his mother would say (his mother is a strong evangelical Christian) and then about what I would say (he described me as somebody who is always mingling with everybody) to his dilemma. After some thought, he told his friend's father that he would participate, but that he was not ready to say the prayers. The family hosting him received his decision with joy.

Carlos Andrés arrived home the next evening and could not stop speaking about this experience. It was clear that he had been very close to God. Two months after the Hanukkah experience, Carlos Andrés came into our bedroom and with tears in his eyes told his mother and me that he wanted to be baptized. In his testimony to the congregation before his baptism, he witnessed to the presence and pull of God in his life at the Hanukkah celebration at his friend's house. He also said that he wanted to study more about God in other people's faiths. I am still praying and wrestling with my son's unique process of commitment to the Christian faith through a Jewish ritual. Consequently, *theologies and practices of mission in the twenty-first century need to address the challenge of people of other faiths, not only in the non-Western world, but in North America as well. We are challenged to find the complex affinities between our faith and other faiths, as well as the distinctions and peculiarities of each. This task will help us discern and develop a missiology in the context of religious diversity.*

From Testimonies to a Statement of Faith and Mission

My missiology is informed by my biography. I am an evangelical Christian by the grace of God, not by choice. God comes to my life as an overwhelming reality encompassing all the dimensions of my life. I do not have the truth. The truth has me.

I am also a Christian of the third world. My biography is about multiple and interpenetrated realities and identities. These realities are political, religious, social, anthropological, historical, and theological in nature. They are about struggles for justice and self-determination; about religious cross-fertilization; about class conflict; about intercultural identity; about a painful and subversive memory, a confusing present, and an uncertain future; about violent cultural encounters and multicultural coexistence; and about God's presence, activity, and hope in this conflicting reality. I am an expression of the encounter of these multiple and interpenetrated realities.

My identity as an evangelical Christian, therefore, is also interpenetrated. Being an evangelical, third world Christian missiologist is about living at the border, fluctuating between the truth and the realities that have me. It is about being a Christian missiologist with all the contradictions, paradoxes, uncertainties and complexities that shape the life of Christians in Africa, Asia, and Latin America. It is also about searching for insights and perspectives that can help my community discern God's purpose and activity in our histories. It is also about doing, about embodying and risking and living the faith.

The border, therefore, is not only my social location, it is also my spiritual location for searching and doing. I am as I search and do; I search as I do and am; I do as I am and search. At the *border* I discover the following:

Christian mission is the recognition, participation, and proclamation by the Christian community of God's activity in the world. As an evangelical Christian, I believe and confess that the birth, life, ministry, death, and resurrection of Jesus are the critical embodiment, the critical point of reference, the vector to understand, act, and live in God's way and to coparticipate in God's activity. As an evangelical Christian at the border I find myself, through and in the power and guidance of the Holy Spirit, discerning, grappling, struggling, and celebrating the multiple ways in which God's activity is embodied, shaped, and understood in a context different from my own. As I cross the border to a strange space, I do it with trepidation and commitment. Trepidation, because I know that God's activity antecedes and is greater than my Christian witness. Commitment, because I can only share God's activity in my life and in the life of my community. Trepidation, because I know that my faith has been communicated many times with violence and arrogance. Commitment, because I know that my faith is not about violence and arrogance, but about peace and reconciliation. Trepidation, because I know I may find new ways of believing, speaking, and confessing God. Commitment, because I know that others may find new ways of believing, speaking, and confessing God. Trepidation, because I am risking my religious identity. Commitment, because risk is natural at the border and because proclaiming and living the Christian faith is about risk. Trepidation, because I am walking on sacred ground. Commitment, because I know that the Spirit of Christ accompanies me.

NOTES

    1. Justo L. González, *Santa Biblia: The Bible through Hispanic Eyes* (Nashville: Abingdon, 1996), 84.

2. Rubem Alves, "From Paradise to Desert," in *Third World Liberation Theologies*, ed. Deane William Ferm (Maryknoll, N.Y.: Orbis, 1986), 99.

3. Ibid., 100.

4. Most exceptions are from African-American, Asian American, or Native American groups.

5. Roberto S. Goizueta, *Caminemos con Jesus* (Maryknoll, N.Y.: Orbis, 1995), 153–54.

6. For a thorough account of this missiological situation in the West, see Lesslie Newbigin, *The Gospel in a Pluralistic Society* (Grand Rapids: Eerdmans, 1989).

7. See Stephen Bevans, *Models of Contextual Theology* (Maryknoll, N.Y.: Orbis, 1992), 47–80.

8. Charles Taylor, *Multiculturalism and "the Politics of Recognition"* (Princeton, N.J.: Princeton University Press, 1992), 31–41.

9. Ibid., 31.

10. Goizueta, *Caminemos con Jesus,* 154.

11. Alan Neely, *Christian Mission: A Case Study Approach* (Maryknoll, N.Y.: Orbis, 1995), 3.

12. Justo González has written a provocative article entitled "Hanging on an Empty Cross: The Hispanic Mainline Experience" in *Protestantes/Protestants,* ed. David Maldonado Jr. (Nashville: Abingdon, 1999), 293–303.

13. See Andrew Walls, *The Missionary Movement in Christian History* (Maryknoll, N.Y.: Orbis, 1996); Kwame Bediako, *Theology and Identity* (Oxford: Regnum, 1992) and *Christianity in Africa* (Edinburgh: Edinburgh University Press, 1995); Dana Roberts, "Shifting Southward: Global Christianity since 1945," *International Bulletin of Missionary Research* 24 (2000): 50–58.

14. Carlos F. Cardoza-Orlandi, "Nos llamaron: mulatos, fiesteros, pero redimibles: Antropología misionera y protestantismo en Puerto Rico," *Apuntes* 14, no. 4 (Winter 1994): 109.

From Missionary to Missiologist at the Margins

Three Decades
of Transforming Mission

SHERRON K. GEORGE

I chose the title for this essay as a tribute to South African David J. Bosch, whose monumental work, *Transforming Mission: Paradigm Shifts in Theology of Mission,* enabled me to integrate my missionary experience and theological reflections with a biblical, ecumenical, global, and contextual perspective. Bosch uses *transforming* with two nuances. First, God's mission transforms people. During the twenty-three years I spent in Brazil as a Presbyterian mission worker, I was transformed in innumerous ways. Among other things, I discovered a new paradigm, a new perspective, a new identity, and a new attitude for mission. The content of this essay will portray the process and describe the results of my transformation and discoveries. I also trust that God has used my life, witness, teaching, preaching, and writing to transform other people, both in Brazil and in the United States.

Second, as people are transformed, so too is their theology of mission and the ways they define and practice it. One factor in my decision to leave Brazil in 1995 was my own missiology. I left as a statement that mission in Brazil has journeyed through the four stages G. Thompson Brown enumerates in his book, *Presbyterians in World Mission*: (1) the mission of the U.S. "sending church," (2) the establishment of a "missionary church" in another land, (3) the growth of the national church and the corresponding decrease of the foreign mission, and (4) the mutual "church to church" integration in a "church-based mission." Brown then asks, "Is it time for a new model?"[1] I think we have been suffering the birth pains of a new model of mission in Brazil for half a century. My struggle in Brazil was to be a midwife of the new model.

Mission has been transformed around the world by former "mission fields" that have become mission sending agents. Strong autonomous denominations and local churches throughout the world are doing mission in six continents. The churches in each nation have primary responsibility for mission in that country. This is stated well by Darrell Guder in *Missional Church:* "A now global church recognize[s] that the church of any place bears missional calling and responsibility for its own place as well as for distant places. The church of every place is a mission-sending church, and the place of every church is a mission-receiving place."[2]

What is the new role of the Presbyterian Church (U.S.A.) in this configuration? What does it mean for the United States to be a "mission-receiving place"? In response to this challenge, I discerned a call and left Brazil to participate in God's mission in the United States. My contribution is to facilitate, advise, encourage, and guide U.S. churches in global awareness and local-global mission endeavors as a part of God's mission project.

Another book that has helped me articulate this twofold understanding of transforming mission is Anthony Gittins's *Bread for the Journey: A Mission of Transformation and the Transformation of Mission.* He defines transformational missional attitudes and spirituality as dialogical, incarnational, and respectful of the cultural identity of others, going beyond the binary mentality of "us" and "them."[3] He calls for "mission in reverse," or two-way mission in which transformation and the exchange of gifts are mutual.

I have been transformed by my mission involvement in Brazil. Now I am teaching others the lesson I have learned, that mission is being (and must be!) transformed. I summarize that lesson by describing (1) a new paradigm of mutuality, (2) a new perspective of solidarity, and (3) a new identity of marginality, and conclude by pointing to a new attitude of bold humility to carry us into the future.

Mutuality: A New Paradigm (the 1970s)

As a young person I read missionary biographies and listened avidly to mission speakers. My youth group encountered inspiration through interaction at the Montreat Global Mission Conference. It was at that Presbyterian retreat center in the mountains of North Carolina that I committed myself to participate in God's mission. I responded one night to an invitation and prayed a simple prayer: "God, I am willing to be a missionary if that is Your will for me." At Belhaven College in Jackson, Mississippi, my interest in missions heightened. In 1972, while I was completing my M.A.

in English at the University of North Carolina and serving my home church as director of Christian education, God opened the door for me to go to Brazil as a Mission Coworker under the appointment of the Presbyterian Board of World Missions. I remember one point from Jule Spach's sermon on Acts 13 at my commissioning service in Montreat: it is not the church or the board that sends us; it is God's Spirit who sends us into mission. There was my first basic building block of sound missiology—*missio Dei*. I had opened myself to the leading of the Spirit, and God had sovereignly and mysteriously directed and confirmed my call.

I was overwhelmed when I arrived in Campinas. I had never lived in a city as large with so many vibrant sights, sounds, and smells. My first challenge was to learn Portuguese so that I could communicate with ease. Language is a very important symbol of identity for a people and mastering it is a sign of respect. I would walk several blocks every morning to the language school, passing a huge block that housed the Presbyterian Seminary of the South. I was too busy savoring the flowers and experimenting with my new language to dream that someday I would teach in that seminary. After nine months of daily Portuguese classes, weekly guitar lessons, wonderful discoveries of fruits and vegetables in the open air market, and fascinating trips to Brasilia and Rio de Janeiro, I packed my new yellow Volkswagen Beetle and headed west to Dourados in southwest Brazil near the border with Paraguay.

During my first two terms, I worked in fourteen small rural congregations scattered in small towns around Dourados at the invitation of the Presbyterian Church of Brazil (IPB), a denomination started when Ashbel Green Simonton, the first Presbyterian missionary, arrived in Rio de Janeiro in 1859. When I first arrived in Dourados, there were several other Presbyterian missionaries from whom I learned and received support. As a consultant in Christian education, I spent many hours driving on dusty roads, enjoying hospitality in simple homes, hearing stories, teaching, and leading services in churches and homes. Countless persons received, respected, nurtured, supported, and taught me. The warm, open, gracious, and informal Latin American culture was different from anything I had ever known. Over the years, the profuse Brazilian hospitality showered upon me, the demonstrations of sacrificial love offered to me in meals and gifts, the millions of hugs and kisses on the cheeks, and the sincere expressions of faith and friendship offered with passion and creativity have taught me that the practice of hospitality is the essence of church, evangelism, and mission.

I came to know the deep faith of the rural Brazilian Christians and experienced a welcoming evangelistic church. The church's zeal for evangelization and desire for leadership development captivated me. In 1979, I penned my first text in Portuguese, *A Igreja Evangelistica* (*The Evangelistic Church*), to train emerging lay leaders in fledgling village congregations.

When I began my second term in Dourados, all of the expatriate missionaries were gone, except for medical specialists Alan and Alma Gordon. I inherited the large missionary manse and made an important missiological decision. I wanted only Brazilians to live with me so that my home and lifestyle would increasingly become more inculturated. I worked with the *one* ordained Brazilian pastor, Joaquim Bezerra Bonfim, responsible for the fourteen congregations, and two Brazilian lay evangelists. Later, PC(USA) missionaries Paul and Dell Coblentz joined our team. My close relationships with Joaquim and Mercedes Bonfim, Dalva and Avelino Rezende, and single evangelists Laureci Garcia and Rodrigo Cardoso in my first term had laid the foundations for mutuality.

During the summers I would invite students from the Edward Lane Bible Institute in Patrocinio, Minas Gerais, as well as youth from the region, to help me lead Vacation Bible Schools in each of the fourteen congregations. They stayed with me, we prepared the materials, and then we divided into two teams. Each week I would drop one team off at one congregation and then go as part of the second team to another congregation. One of those students was Dirce Naves from the state of Minas Gerais. After her graduation from the Institute, she worked with me a second summer in 1976, and has been working with me ever since. Dirce has enabled me to see Brazil and the United States through penetratingly honest and candid Brazilian eyes. In our relationship as mission coworkers in Brazil and in the United States, I hope we have become a model of mutuality in mission. My ministry both in Brazil and here in the United States would not be the same without Dirce's gifts and contributions. Because of her insights and perspectives into Brazilian and U.S. culture, I have been transformed into a bicultural person.

However, this has been an incremental process. Absorption in one particular social location can lead to isolation from the larger ecclesiastical, political, social, and economic picture. I chose not to own a television in the 1970s, and, like my rural parishioners, was oblivious to the situation under the military government in Brazil's cities. At first I subscribed to *Time* magazine, but when my interest shifted from microanalysis to macroanalysis, I changed my news magazine subscription to Brazil's *Veja*. I started to become "conscienticized" to Brazilian social analysis and cognizant of Presbyterian church politics.

I began to experience mutuality as a result of a decade of immersion and friendships in southwest Brazil. I was instructed by the thread of mutuality that runs through Romans, beginning with Paul's desire to be "mutually encouraged among you through the mutual faith of both you and me" (Rom. 1:11–12).

The results of my transformation can be described as "mission-in-reverse." Mission leader Claude-Marie Barbour defines it this way:

> [M]ission-in-reverse teaches that the minister can and should learn from the people ministered to—including, and perhaps especially, from the poor and marginalized people. By taking these people seriously, by listening to them, personal relationships are developed, and the dignity of the people is enhanced. Such presence to people is seen as necessarily allowing them to be the leaders in the relationship.[4]

In my early ingenuous days I assumed that all mission relationships were horizontal two-way partnerships based on love and respect, in which the gifts of all partners were valued without creating dependencies or humiliating anyone. Later I realized that mutuality is hard work. Unless we humbly, intentionally, and patiently build dialogical relationships and practice two-way mission, U.S. Christians easily fall into one-way mission activities that are demeaning for the people we seek to serve. I gradually learned that more important than anything we build, teach, or give is who we are and what attitude we have in relating to other people, religions, and cultures.

One-way, hierarchical, dependency-prone, control-oriented mission relationships might be called mission, but I do not think they are God's mission. Any mission practice that starts from assumptions of superiority of *doers* and inferiority of *receivers* is not really mission, but imperialistic aid. While the theory of partnership, equality, and mutuality between older and younger churches goes back to the nineteenth and early twentieth centuries, the gap or transition between vision and practice has often been discouraging.

At a conference of the Presbyterian Church in the United States (PCUS) held in Montreat in 1962, the Board of World Missions, according to G. Thompson Brown, hailed "equal partnership" as the flagship of a new day of church to church mission. However, Brown also points out that the transition was not easy, for the "missionary organization had to die," and that "[n]ational church leaders found it difficult to cope with the strange ways of church bureaucracies in the United States."[5]

How long does the transition take? How far are we on the journey? Has the vision become reality? During the 1980s, Missao Presbiteriana *no* Brasil (Presbyterian Mission *in* Brazil), an organization made up of

PC(USA) missionaries, was transformed into the Missao Presbiteriana *do* Brasil (Presbyterian Mission *of* Brazil), whose members are representatives from two Brazilian Presbyterian denominations and the PC(USA). As president during this organizational transition, I experienced resistance, ambivalence, and conflict with some missionaries and realized that we still have a long way to go to achieve true mutuality.

Solidarity: A New Perspective (the 1980s)

After two terms of immersion in Brazilian culture and the church's ministry in Dourados, I returned to the United States and studied for two years at Columbia Theological Seminary in Decatur, Georgia, where I gained new perspectives on biblical interpretation, theology, spirituality, worship, and ministry. I opted for the Doctor of Ministry-in-Sequence Program and made plans to do my project in Brazil.

In 1982, I began my third term by moving over two thousand miles from Dourados to the city of Manaus to work with two presbyteries of the Presbyterian Church of Brazil (IPB) as an educational consultant and professor. My Brazilian coworker, Dirce Naves, and I taught custom-designed courses for teachers in nine churches, and I taught missions and Christian education in the lay institute. I challenged the students to be God's agents in evangelizing the unreached peoples in the Amazon Basin and to be in solidarity with their neighbors along the rivers and the poor fishers in houses on stilts in the city. In dialogical collaboration with my students I wrote *A Igreja Ensinadora* (*The Teaching Church*), which combined my interests in Christian education, theology, and contextualization, and became the core of my doctor of ministry project. In Manaus I was the only PC(USA) mission worker. I enjoyed effective and intellectually stimulating collegial relationships with Brazilian pastors, students, lay leaders, and church members. I also was mentored by mature friends, including my on-site doctor of ministry advisor, Rev. Joao Chrysostomo Jr.

Time passed rapidly as I experienced tremendous receptivity and energy in teaching and developed many significant relationships. Years later I gained a new perspective on the significance of my experience in Manaus. In 1999, I returned to Manaus for a visit. Traveling with a group from St. Andrews-Covenant Presbyterian Church (Wilmington, North Carolina), we joined my former student, Nonato dos Santos, pastor of the growing Petropolis Presbyterian Church, on a visit by boat to three of the seven communities the Petropolis Presbyterian Church was evangelizing along the river. It took us fourteen hours by boat from Manaus to reach the first community! There are nine thousand such communities in the state of Amazonas. Only nineteen hundred have churches, which leaves more than seven thousand unreached communities. As I watched Rev. Santos and Cleildo, a lay evangelist, reach out in solidarity with the river folks, my heart was touched and challenged.

After returning to Manaus from the river trip, I learned about the ministry of another congregation, the Presbyterian Church of Manaus. Rev. Chrysostomo and Rev. Jose Joao Mesquita informed me that the two-thousand-member church has three boats that are used in their ministry in the fourteen new church developments and ten preaching points they support in rural jungle areas in the state. As soon as it is feasible, those churches will become self-supporting with their own ministers. What a joy to return to Manaus fifteen years after teaching mission there and witness the growth of dynamic churches with a clear mission focus and strategy!

In 1983, I accepted the insistent invitation of the Caiua Indian Mission in Dourados to teach at the new Felipe Landes Bible Institute. Dirce and I moved back two thousand miles to the southwest and helped reorganize that program, which had started with all indigenous Brazilians from several tribes, but hailed only European-Brazilians when we arrived. We invited all of them to find other places to study, revamped the curriculum, adapted the school calendar to the agricultural year, and consequently saw many indigenous Christians enroll. Many of them now have graduated and serve as evangelists with their own tribes and with other tribes. My involvement with indigenous Brazilians led me another step down the road toward solidarity.

In my research for my dissertation on "Contextualizing Christian Education in Brazil," I encountered Paulo Freire, one of the persons who has most profoundly impacted me. I was enthralled by his *Pedagogia do Oprimido* (Pedagogy of the Oppressed). He introduced me to the concept of *conscientizacao* (conscientization or consciousness-raising) and helped me explore with the oppressed the structural causes of their condition. His proposal for a reflective dialogical "liberating education" transformed me as an educator and taught me to treat all human beings as subjects-agents of transformation.

After completing my final year at Columbia Seminary and being ordained by Salem Presbytery in 1986, the Independent Presbyterian Church of Brazil (IPIB) invited me to teach mission and Christian education at their seminary in Londrina, a lovely city in southern Brazil only three hundred miles from Dourados. There students and professors challenged me both as a citizen of the richest country in the world and as a missionary from a dominating culture. They denounced individualism and insisted on "doing theology from below." My colleague Julio Zabatiero, a liberation theologian, taught me a fresh hermeneutical approach to the scriptures (which Robert McAfee Brown demonstrates in his book *Unexpected News: Reading the Bible with Third World Eyes*). My new discoveries led me to read avidly Brazilians Rubem Alves and Leonardo Boff, Latin American evangelicals Orlando Costas and C. Rene Padilla, and Roman Catholics Gustavo Gutierrez and Segundo Galilea. As my pedagogy had been transformed by Freire, so my theology and missiology were turned upside down, especially when I started reading and listening to Boff, Costas, and Galilea. I only knew mission as done by the rich, but Galilea suggested that mission can best be done out of poverty. The poor understand and practice solidarity with one another. In *Christ Outside the Gate: Mission Beyond Christendom,* Costas proclaimed the United States as a mission field, a "new Macedonia" for Third World Christians, and offered an agenda for evangelization in the United States in the 1980s.

I joined my students and colleagues as they reflected critically on North American mission and church, stood in solidarity with the poor and marginalized, contextually analyzed Brazilian church and society, and created a Brazilian liturgy and theology from their perspective and with their aesthetic forms. My continuing conversion and radical transformation accelerated. I followed Brazil's outstanding evening world news and well-done *telenovelas* on my television, carefully read *Veja* magazine, passionately discussed Brazilian political and economic issues, and began to view and interpret world and U.S. actions from the perspective of the southern hemisphere. At the same time, as the first ordained woman most of them had known, I stood in special solidarity and advocacy with our few female students, insisting on gender inclusive language, stretching the boundaries that limited the space and authority of women, and striving for the day when the IPIB would vote for the ordination of women, which happened in 1999.

By the end of the 1980s, I was ready for the first articulation of my missiology. I used the dialogical method of Paulo Freire and, in creative conversation with twelve students in a mission class, wrote the book *A Igreja Missionaria* (*The Missionary Church*). In the process, they caught, owned, refined, enhanced, and practiced my vision of the local-global missional church.

I saw Brazilians practice solidarity and I joined them. Later I reflected, researched, and tried to name and define solidarity. Solidarity requires taking seriously "the ideas and experience of others on their own terms" and suspending one's "personal, cultural, and religious ideas and practices to listen for the experience and meanings of others."[6] Solidarity is participation "in the people's struggles and problems, as well as in their aspirations and hopes."[7] In order to be in solidarity with others we must identify and transcend personal boundaries and "move through them and allow ourselves to be pulled, perhaps with some resistance, by those on the other side."[8] A biblical example of solidarity is the incarnation of Jesus, "who, though he was in the form of God, did not regard equality with God as something to be exploited, but emptied himself, taking the form of a slave, being born in human likeness. And being found in human form, he humbled himself" (Phil. 2:6–8, NRSV).

While visiting Brazil in 1999, I purchased two of Leonardo Boff's latest books, *A Aguia e a Galinha* (*The Eagle and the Chicken*) and *O Despertar da Aguia* (*The Awakening of the Eagle*). He uses a story by Ghanaian educator James Aggrey about an injured eagle who assumed the identity of a chicken after living with chickens. Only after persuasive coaching did he soar again as an eagle. Boff sees this as a metaphor of the dialectical nature of the human condition in which something of an eagle and a chicken are in every person. The eagle in everyone must be freed. The fact that some are forced to live only the chicken dimension reveals the loss of respect for human beings, human solidarity, and compassion in today's world. Brazilians have taught me that the key to solidarity is compassion, which includes empathy, sharing the feelings of the other, standing emotionally with the other, affective identification with the cause of the other, and passionate advocacy on behalf of the other.

Marginality: A New Identity (the 1990s)

I was quite content teaching in the IPIB seminary in Londrina when I received an invitation to join the faculty of the IPB Seminary of the South in Campinas, the oldest and largest Presbyterian seminary in Brazil. I was the first mission worker they had invited back since Richard Shaull left in the 1960s and the IPB unilaterally broke its formal relationship with the newly reunited PC(USA) in 1983. I would be the first ordained woman to teach there. For these reasons, I accepted the challenges to design a graduate program in Christian education and to teach in the bachelor of theology program. I began the new decade in Campinas at the seminary by which I had walked daily when I first arrived in Brazil in 1972.

The graduate program in Christian education started with a class of twelve very talented students who caught a radically new vision of Christian education, based on Paulo Freire's pedagogy. With them I wrote my next book, a complete revision of *A Igreja Ensinadora* (*The Teaching Church*), with expanded biblical, theological, historical, and pedagogical foundations. Brazilians readily comprehend holistic education of mind, body, and spirit, and excel in didactic creativity and religious imagination. The level of mutual friendships that I developed with colleagues and students such as Dinayde Ferraz, Ana Maria Rocha, Rev. Silas de Campos, Samuel and Cilei Kohn, Dr. Eduardo Lane, Maria Maia, and Cida Dutra has no parallel in my life journey.

After receiving much and giving what I could for twenty-three years, writing four books in Portuguese, preaching in many churches and at three seminary commencements, and serving as professor at several institutions, I sensed God calling me in 1995 to return to the United States. Dirce Naves accompanied me to continue her participation in the Mission to the U.S.A. program in hospital and senior citizen chaplaincy, and so that I would not lose the daily Latin perspective "from below."

Because of the vision and passion that I obtained in Brazil as a result of my transformation through mission-in-reverse, I feel that I now have something important to share with Christians in the United States. My experience of solidarity with Latin Americans and with all who are marginalized has given me a new way of perceiving American culture and church. I view myself as a marginal, bicultural Christian, a member of the global faith community passionately committed to God's mission.

I served as missionary-in-residence with the Worldwide Ministries Division in Louisville, Kentucky, for one year to coordinate preparations for the Year with Latin Americans. On July 31, 1996, I ended my service as a PC(USA) mission worker, and on August 1 assumed my new mission post as assistant professor of evangelism and mission at Austin Presbyterian Theological Seminary in Texas. God called me to dream, prepare, plan, empower, and envision the participation of Christians in the United States in God's local-global mission in the new millennium in a changed and changing culture, society, world, and church. As I entered the strange new world of Austin Seminary, still intensely feeling reverse culture shock, I wondered how I might be God's faithful agent of transformation and lead others to practice and experience transforming mission-in-reverse at this moment and space in history.

A marvelous feature of the Austin Seminary curriculum is a required course on mission and evangelism, which I teach every spring semester. I begin by describing the changes in church and society in the modern/ postmodern context. It is hard for some people in the United States to understand that the place of the mission field has changed and is now everywhere, that the position and influence of the mainstream Protestant churches in the United States have become marginal, that the reasons people choose and attend churches have changed, and that approaches to mission and evangelism must be different today.

The main part of the course focuses on *Transforming Mission* by David Bosch. Students come to understand that the triune God has a saving mission, that God's mission has a church, and that the Bible is a missionary document for a church in mission with others. As we journey through historical mission paradigms, it becomes obvious that we must move beyond models of paternalism, colonialism, and imperialism. Bosch points to an "emerging ecumenical missionary paradigm," which includes justice, evangelism, contextualization, liberation, and witness to and dialogue with peoples of other faiths. I emphasize mutuality, solidarity, and marginality as important components in the new paradigm and seek to practice them in the classroom with dialogue, respect, and compassion. Students do ten hours of mission practice that pushes them beyond one-way mission and engages them in working together with others as equals.

As I began to visit, teach, and preach in churches in the United States, I was shocked at how monocultural and monoracial Presbyterian congregations are. I was accustomed to racially mixed families, communities, and churches in Brazil. I rejoiced when the 208th General Assembly of the PC(USA) adopted a goal of increasing our racial ethnic membership from 4.7 percent to 10 percent by the year 2005 and to 20 percent by the year 2010. In the preparations for the Year with Latin Americans, I realized that to become a multicultural church, the PC(USA) must work more closely with our Latin American constituency, our 223 Hispanic congregations. The proximity of Texas to Mexico was a key factor in attracting me to Austin Seminary. Spanish was the official language in what is now Texas (and six other states) before English was spoken. For generations, Mexican-Americans have molded the culture of the Southwest. I was shocked again when I discovered the prejudice and discrimination against Latinos by Anglos in Texas, the struggle of Latino voices and churches in the Southwest, and Austin Seminary's history of frustrated Hispanic initiatives and its present low Latino student representation.

In my relationships with our few Hispanic students, I began to comprehend their painful experiences. I also found myself developing bonds with our international students and seeing life in the U.S. churches and the seminary through their eyes. God's mission involves sending and receiving. When we warmly receive new immigrants and students from the global church and learn to look at the world's needs and our culture through their eyes, we are engaged in mission. The greatest vitality for mission and church growth today comes from countries such as South Korea, China, Nigeria, Kenya, and Brazil. The PC(USA) has a new role as learner and follower in the global faith community.

Marginal voices in my classes, especially the elective seminars, have taken me to a deeper level of transformation. In my course, "Toward a Multicultural Church in a Multicultural Society," we discover from Jung Young Lee's *Marginality: The Key to Multicultural Theology* that persons who live in two cultures are neither one, nor the other; they do not fully belong to either. In other words, bicultural persons are at the margin of both cultures, in between two worlds while simultaneously in both one and the other. When we assume the perspective of marginality in contrast to the position of power and centrality, we emulate the model of the self-emptying Jesus and become a servant church of reconciliation, healing, and global liberation.

Putting myself and my students in situations where we learn from global Christian colleagues is an important facet of my practice as a professor of mission. In December 1996, Darrell Guder and I took twenty seminary students from eight seminaries in the United States and Canada to Salvador, Brazil, to participate in the World Council of Churches' Conference on World Mission and Evangelism. This was the centerpiece of a course entitled, "The Gospel in Diverse Cultures: Missiological Interaction with the Conference on World Mission and Evangelism." In our contacts with the global church and the Brazilian context, issues of contextualization, syncretism, proselytism, and vehement criticism of North Atlantic Christians were paramount.

In April 1998, I participated in the Cook Travel Seminar of the Presbyterian Church (U.S.A.) in China. In the rapidly growing postdenominational Chinese church there are more than eight million Roman Catholics, twelve million Protestants, and seventeen Protestant seminaries. Our group visited seminaries in Shanghai, Hangzhou, and Nanjing, where PC(USA) and Chinese professors gave papers on witness in context. We met with students, professors, pastors, and leaders of the China Christian Council and Three-Self Movement. One of the highlights was a conversation with Bishop K. H. Ting in his home. Our guide and translator, Melissa Man-Hong Lin, later came to Austin Seminary for a year of graduate study during which she enriched our community with her delightful presence and profound insights.

I offered a course during the 1999 doctor of ministry January term on

"Solidarity and Mutuality: A New Paradigm for Mission and Evangelism," most of which took place in Cuba. The Rev. Dr. Carlos Emilio Ham of the Presbyterian-Reformed Church in Cuba and I designed and led the course. The U.S. pastors were overwhelmed with the effusive Latin hospitality and the creative theological depth of the Cuban scholars and pastors who challenged and nurtured us with the presentations of their papers and ministries. When we asked them if it was possible for us to be in solidarity with them, they replied Yes, but only if you first advocate against the immoral U.S. blockade and if you make space in your churches and seminaries to listen to Cuban theologians. In listening to Christians in socialist China and Cuba I learned much about solidarity, which for them is a way of life.

Bold Humility: A New Attitude

After teaching mission in a PC(USA) seminary for several years and reflecting on my twenty-three years of experience as a PC(USA) mission coworker in Brazil, I have come to an astounding conclusion. We lack a clear definition of mission. The old definition of mission as the Western church imperialistically sending missionaries to distant places is no longer viable.

My working definition of mission is this: Mission is everything the local-global church is sent into the world to be and do as a participant in God's mission and every person and gift the local-global church receives in Christ's name and way. The missional practice of the local-global church must be holistic, with activities of evangelism, compassionate service, and social justice. God's loving mission is two-way; it includes both giving and receiving. Every person, religion, and culture has material, intellectual, aesthetic, social, affective, and spiritual values that the other can receive.

I challenge you Presbyterians in the United States to go to the margins, to listen to the marginalized, and to allow God to transform you. May we together move into the future with an attitude that David Bosch terms "bold humility" and "humble boldness."[9]

Humility is the antidote to imperialism and paternalism. One-way mission that considers some to be superior subjects and others to be inferior objects who must be treated with condescension and pity is not *missio Dei*. We must humbly admit that we have made mistakes and that the United States is also a mission field. We must be willing to learn from people who are different from us in our neighborhoods and around the world.

Boldness is needed to recover our evangelistic witness in a society marked by individualism, tolerance, and pluralism. We must relearn, rediscover, or reinvent evangelism and practice it humbly and respectfully but unashamedly. We must boldly move beyond mere social service to costly social justice and compassionate evangelistic witness.

Mutuality, solidarity, marginality, and *bold humility* may sound like so much mission jargon to some. For me, they represent the reality of God's awesome power in my life and in my world. I pray that these reflections contribute to a deeper and broader understanding of mission. May God's mission fuel our passion and lead us to the margins where, by God's grace, we may be mutually transformed.

NOTES

1. G. Thompson Brown, *Presbyterians in World Mission* (Decatur, Ga.: CTS Press, 1995), 47–50.

2. Darrell L. Guder, ed., *Missional Church* (Grand Rapids: Eerdmans, 1998), 81.

3. Anthony Gittins, *Bread for the Journey: A Mission of Transformation and the Transformation of Mission* (Maryknoll, N.Y.: Orbis, 1993), 16–17.

4. Quoted in Gittens, *Bread for the Journey,* 56.

5. Brown, *Presbyterians in World Mission,* 44.

6. Charles R. Foster, *Embracing Diversity: Leadership in Multicultural Congregations* (Bethesda, Md.: Alban Institute, 1997), 68–69.

7. Tetsunao Yamamori, et al., eds., *Serving with the Poor in Latin America,* (Monrovia, Calif.: MARC, 1997), 111.

8. Gittins, *Bread for the Journey,* 150.

9. David J. Bosch, *Transforming Mission: Paradigm Shifts in Theology of Mission* (Maryknoll, N.Y.: Orbis, 1991), 489.

PART III

Mission in a Pluralist Society

Among the Believers

Muslims and Christians in the Dar al-Islam

STANLEY H. SKRESLET

I took my first plunge into the world of Islam more than a quarter century ago. After a brief stop in Istanbul, Bible professor John Anderson led our group of Lewis and Clark College undergraduates further east, to Iran, where we would spend nearly six months studying Farsi, Persian history and culture, and the religion of Islam. Lifelong friendships were forged in that experience, and in some cases, faith was tested. For all of us, this was an eye-opening initiation into one of the world's most brilliant cultural and religious traditions.

Iran in the early 1970s was a third world country on the cusp of profound changes. In keeping with the mood of the previous decade, the star of development's promise still beckoned brightly in the Western sky. An extended effort to transform Iran's traditional ways, symbolically summed up in the Shah's ten-year-old White Revolution, appeared ready to take off. The way forward seemed to require a diminished public role for Islam, a sidelining of religious leaders in favor of Western-trained technocrats, and an embrace of "modern" norms of social behavior and education. This did not mean throwing overboard everything from Iran's past, however. A momentous rummage through the nation's cultural attic was underway, with pride of place given to a few items selected from Iran's pre-Islamic heritage. Chief among these was the monarchy itself, which, on the occasion of the Shah's coronation in 1968, had been lavishly celebrated as the enduring and distinctively Persian center of the new cultural matrix then under construction.

Not long after our study group arrived in the fall of 1973, a palpable surge in the forces of history seemed to lend confirmation to the wisdom of the Shah's modernizing strategy. In the aftermath of the

October War between Egypt and Israel, a successful OPEC embargo of petroleum exports to the West led to an immediate and dramatic spike in Iran's oil revenues, soon followed by additional sharp increases, after a half century or so of almost flat wholesale pricing. The tide of easy profits that began to wash over the region produced in some quarters an almost giddy sense of anticipation, an ardent hopefulness about the future of Iran and its Arab neighbors. Ambitious planners of Western-style development in Tehran now had an enormous source of capital at hand to finance the Shah's vision. The regime had only to revise its timetable for Iran's leap into modernity.

Rapid and radical change, of course, did come to Iran in the 1970s, but it was of an entirely different character than that forecast earlier in the decade. The revolution that swept over the country was religious, not secular, led by ascetics, not entrepreneurs or state policymakers, and it unfolded within a conceptual framework shaped essentially by Shari'a law and the turbulent history of early Shi'ism. Subsequent political events and the rhetoric of the revolution's leadership suggested to many in the West that this was a simple struggle between the worst kind of reactionary religion and progressive modernism, a backward-looking medievalism in conflict with universal human aspirations for freedom, democracy, and human rights. One need not be a Middle East expert or specialist in Islam to suspect that these categories did not do full justice to the complex religious and social transformation that overtook Iran at the end of the 1970s.

I did not realize it at the time, but during my brief sojourn in Iran I had been exposed to a living illustration of missiological reality at work. A particular religious heritage, in this case Shi'ite Islam, was contending uneasily with at least two sets of social values that lay outside its immediate field of view: the post-Enlightenment secularism of the West and a broad Persian cultural tradition from which its pre-Islamic religious elements had been largely stripped. This interaction did not take place in the abstract but in a dynamic geopolitical context defined by powerful political and economic factors such as the Cold War, the Shah's ambition for Iran to be a regional superpower in the Gulf, the Arab-Israeli conflict, and the politics of big petroleum. Yet another critical social factor was the indignation felt by many Iranians that various Western colonial powers had ruthlessly pursued their own advantage at the expense of Iran's national interests by dominating its internal affairs for much of the twentieth century.

Many of the Muslims I got to know best in Iran found themselves personally challenged by the historically significant struggle swirling around them to define Iran's identity. On the one hand, individual Iranian Muslims had to evaluate and respond to the ruling elite's proposition that religious allegiance could and ought to be subsumed within broader cultural and social values, some of which might be borrowed from abroad. At the same time, increasingly strident voices of protest, like that of the exiled Ayatollah Khomeini, were insisting that only an invigorated and assertive Islam could stand up to the corrosive and irreligious forces of "westoxification" that threatened to dissolve the very foundations of Iran's Muslim identity.

On reflection later, the dilemma of my Muslim friends suggested to me something of the same problem Christian students of mission routinely face when trying to understand how the gospel must enter into tangled networks of cultures set in specific historical circumstances. Christians, too, sometimes have to make difficult choices about how to express religious faith, especially in the public arena, and to think carefully about the layers of culture that both mediate and condition the meaning of religious words and acts. I came to realize that Muslims and Christians share many of the same questions about faith and culture. What deeply rooted customs of this particular people and place are compatible with faith and what is irremediably foreign to it? Is it enough that religious convictions merely season a community's sense of itself, or should one expect the faith of the majority to define national purpose in obvious ways? Can a society willingly identified by a dominant creed nevertheless make room for those outside the religious mainstream? Are the freedoms of modern secular life faith's ally or foe?

A large part of my short time in Iran consisted of formal study undertaken in conjunction with organized field trips to archaeological sites and historically important places and buildings. This was a marvelous way to be introduced to a proud culture and living religious tradition about which few Americans (myself included, at the time) know anything at all. Our group had the opportunity to experience urban life in Tehran, but also to live for an extended time in Shiraz, the fabled city of poets Hafez and Sa'adi that was just a short distance from Persepolis, the ceremonial palace-city of Darius the Great and Xerxes. Other trips took us to less accessible regions of the country, including the eastern desert cities of Kerman and Yazd, plus the gulf region near Abadan. An individual research project on childrearing practices put me in contact with more than a dozen families in Fars province, split between city dwellers and the nomadic Qashqa'i tribe. Finally, two different stays in Isfahan, a spectacular city reputed in medieval times to be "half the world," still represent for me the summit of my encounter with a Muslim aesthetic.

Famous mosques, desolate fire temples perched starkly at the edge of the desert, impressive ruins of Achaemenian power, primitive barrel vaults and early forms of the squinch—such are the subjects that naturally dominate the extant photographic record of a first journey within the *Dar al-Islam*. Other images subsist only in the memory, but some of these mark in a more decisive way a developing missiological self-understanding. One is exemplified by a nearly comic scene of imperfect communication that took place at Persepolis, when a local tourist to the site asked urgently if I had heard about "the scandal of the fire." I immediately wondered how I could have missed the contemporary disaster or latest incident of political intrigue to which he must have been referring. It turned out that he had ancient crimes in mind, the burning of Persepolis having ensued shortly after Alexander the Great's defeat of Darius III, c. 330 B.C.E. What I learned from this brief contact was that historical consciousness perdures in many places around the world to a degree not often felt in American suburban life. More than this, I had been given an inkling of how historical memory can supply, for better or worse, the interpretive templates that subtly but crucially frame our perceptions of the present. Thus for some, erstwhile antipathies between Persians and Greeks neatly parallel later examples of East-West confrontation and so buttress the claim that certain civilizations may be fundamentally incompatible. Likewise, America's behavior abroad is rendered more comprehensible to many when notice is taken of cowboy values and a frontier mentality.

Perhaps the most vital missiological insight I carried back with me from Iran was triggered by the request of a young Tanzanian Muslim with whom I shared housing in Shiraz. Mehdi knew that a part of the curriculum for our college group included a class on Islam and that I was required to prepare a final paper for the course. I chose to do a comparative study of Old Testament figures in the Qur'an. After he asked to see the paper, I realized how important it was to think about the manner in which one writes or speaks about a religious tradition that is not one's own. As he read the paper over the next few days, I thought about what I had written. Was the Qur'anic material handled in a way that was mindful of the community for whom these writings functioned as scripture? Were the characterizations of Muslim belief and practice fair? Was theological critique offered with respect and in a spirit of generosity appropriate to good interfaith relations? In this context and for the future, Mehdi's comments meant much more to me than those of the professor! I have kept the paper as a reminder that every time I am asked to speak in a church setting about Islam, I ought to do so imagining that at least one Muslim would be in attendance. On more than one occasion, that has been a prudent assumption.

Several years later I returned to the Middle East, this time for two years in Egypt as a volunteer teacher sent by The United Presbyterian Church in the U.S.A. My wife and I were both seminary students then in the middle of degree programs in theology at Union Theological Seminary in Virginia. Our beginning mission work put us in two kinds of school environments. One was a high school, which used English as the language of instruction, that had been founded by Presbyterian missionaries and where we taught eleventh-grade English language and literature. The other was a theological seminary that prepared ministers for service in the Egyptian Evangelical (Presbyterian) Church.

We assumed dual roles in each of the institutions to which we had been assigned, becoming both teachers and learners. This was in keeping with the ideological shift that had taken place within mainline Protestantism by the mid-1970s, away from a missionary stance of presumed Western omniscience and toward the practice of mutuality in mission. Our student role was accentuated further by classes in Arabic at the American University in Cairo and a program of reading for our own seminary degree work that focused on Islam and the history of Christianity in Egypt.

Many of the students we taught at the Ramses College for Girls in Cairo were Coptic Orthodox Christians, for whom a deep-felt devotion to their church seemed to come naturally. We were invited to homes and church services on a regular basis. Several times we were able to attend the weekly Bible study conducted by Pope Shenouda III at the Coptic cathedral, just down the street from where we lived. On these occasions, our students took turns translating as Pope Shenouda taught a Wednesday night crowd that rarely numbered less than a thousand.

The fervid and obvious desire of those gathered to grow in their understanding of scripture, as well as the utter seriousness with which the Coptic patriarch took his teaching responsibility, belied the conventional Protestant characterization of Orthodoxy as a tradition with little interest in the Bible or contemporary social realities. Even in this mass context, Pope Shenouda managed to present his ideas with evident pastoral concern for the challenges then faced by his flock, both as modern Egyptians and as Coptic Christians. This was the first time I had ever seen religious education take place that was plainly biblical, assuredly relevant to the needs of those in attendance, and, at the same time, genuinely attentive to the historical experience of the church community. Pope Shenouda often drew from the traditions of the early church in order to explain difficult points in the biblical text. That one could use illustrations from the church fathers and not make the whole enterprise seem hopelessly remote from our own time came as something of a surprise to me. For a second time, believers living in the *Dar al-Islam* had shown me that the historical "ditch" separating our era from antiquity may not be as wide or as deep as it is commonly assumed to be in the modern West.

We were blessed with other opportunities to learn about the Coptic Orthodox Church. A summer in Alexandria made it easy to visit the catacombs there as well as a host of other wonderful sites from the Greco-Roman period. Adventurous colleagues arranged for a visit to St. Menas's monastery, west of the city and deep in the desert, and, in those days, rather less accessible than it is now. A long-time Presbyterian missioner and expert in the field of Coptic musicology, Dr. Martha Roy, introduced us to the complex and self-assured elegance of the Coptic liturgy. An unexpected opening into the world of Coptic Orthodoxy appeared when the dean of the Coptic seminary located at Anba Ruwais offered to tutor us in the Coptic language. This we did for about six months in the traditional way, by writing down bits of the liturgy or other creedal formulae and then taking them home to memorize. The instructor had the only available textbook. I began to appreciate the value of pacing about while studying, a mnemonic activity I had seen students do constantly before exams in both Iran and Egypt.

Part of our introduction to Christianity in Egypt involved learning from Orthodox and Protestant believers (contact with Coptic Catholics would come later) how it felt to live as part of a religious minority under Islam. Unlike in Iran and most of southwest Asia, Egypt's Christian community is sizable, comprising some 12 to 15 percent of the country's total population (estimated at about forty million in the late 1970s but now near seventy million). The origins of this community are not in the West. The Christian tradition came to Egypt from Palestine in the first century of the Common Era, well before the arrival of Islam. By late antiquity, it had become the religion of a majority of Egyptians, whose zealousness for the faith was matched by the profound legacy of Alexandrian theologians such as Origen and Athanasius. Many of Egypt's most original contributions to early Christianity, such as monasticism in its several forms and the desert spirituality that developed with it, continue to inform and enrich a global church today.

A vivid memory from the first full day of our stay in Cairo includes a walk to the Coptic patriarchate, during which we found the grounds full of people although there were no services scheduled at that time. We learned that Pope Shenouda had called for a national day of prayer by the Coptic community in order to protest new regulations from the government that made it easier to convict Egyptian Christians of proselytizing activity. Church leaders feared that these guidelines would be used to intimidate ordinary believers by making it appear that subversive intentions lay behind normal public behavior. A chilling provision allowed for the interrogation of anyone suspected of influencing a Muslim to convert to Christianity.

Only in hindsight would I begin to appreciate the significance of what we had seen that day on the grounds of the Coptic cathedral. We had been given a window through which to observe firsthand evidence of a major cultural transition in progress that had serious potential implications for the Christian community in Egypt. No one could know the eventual outcome of what was happening then, but many of our more experienced colleagues wondered aloud in our hearing about the harbingers of change that multiplied around us. In daily conversations, the still tentative emergence of the Muslim Brotherhood from the shadows of Egypt's public life was under vigorous debate. The long-term consequences of Iran's revolution and the extent to which it might spread within the region remained unclear. Uncertainty also attended Anwar Sadat's opening to the West and his decision to make peace with Israel. In the immediate aftermath of the Camp David agreement, we shared in the excitement of the moment when the president rode in triumph from the airport right down Ramses Street in front of our school to widespread and genuine public acclaim. But questions about what came next hung suspended in the air, as yet unanswered. Would closer ties to the United States prepare the way for the adoption of more Westernized patterns of civil society, presumably to the relief of Egypt's non-Muslim citizens? Could the absence of war with Israel really produce the economic boost promised by the regime, such that poverty's grip on Egypt would finally be loosened and the whole nation together might enjoy a renewal of hope for the future? Others forecast unprecedented strife in response to Sadat's supposed betrayal of Islam by making peace with Israel. In this scenario, the Christian community was in danger of becoming a focus for retaliation aimed against any group that stood to gain from these changes in policy.

Now, of course, we know what has come to pass in the meantime. Sadat had set forces in motion that he would not be able to control. The "believer president," desperate to outflank the ardent Nasserists who still dominated Cairo's intelligentsia and refused to give him their nod of legitimacy, made space in the public arena for Muslim religious activists as an alternative base of support. Unfortunately for him, the newly enfranchised, schooled in the use of power by Iran's revolutionaries and emboldened by the example of Afghan resistance to Soviet hegemony, quickly outgrew their need for presidential patronage.

The late 1970s thus turned out to be the beginning of a more than twenty-year-long period during which Egypt moved unmistakably closer to an Islamist self-understanding. Gamal Abdel Nasser's understanding that Egypt was essentially an Arab nation in which Christians and Muslims could conceivably share in equal parts was pushed aside by the idea that in some fundamental way, Islam defined the character of Egypt's people and culture. The repercussions of this conceptual realignment for Christians in Egypt have been grave. A protracted campaign with many fronts would be waged to Islamicize Egyptian society, with the government having to struggle constantly to retain effective control over key public institutions (such as the professional syndicates, the educational system, and the major religious establishments). An Islamist strategy of destabilization developed, leading to increasingly frequent and deadly outbreaks of religious extremism that often (but not only) targeted Christians and their businesses. More insidiously, subtle pressures on the Christian community and established patterns of relatively modest restrictions that had become an accepted part of life as a religious minority within this part of the *Dar al-Islam* would give way in the 1990s to grosser forms of intimidation.

The Egypt to which we returned in 1989 as Presbyterian mission coworkers had certainly changed. Despite a firm resolve not to cede political power to actors in open opposition to itself, the government had surrendered authority in many other ways. The state apparatus, for instance, was no longer able to assert with the same confidence as before that it was the sole arbiter of what could be published in the country. Prominent Muslim spokesmen such as the Sheikh al-Azhar presumed to pronounce judgment on specific texts already approved by the government for publication or distribution in the country, which resulted in not a few squalid struggles at the annual International Book Fair. The content of school syllabi, set for the entire country by the Ministry of Education, reflected to an increasing degree a more self-consciously Islamic sense of morality (in the choice of literature for the humanities curriculum, for example). At the same time, dress codes for women students had become more conservative. Islamist activists had begun to discover new ways to publicize and articulate their agenda for the nation, the government's near monopoly on the public media notwithstanding. A developing network of social services connected to mosques or Muslim charitable institutions extended its reach and in times of crisis (such as during the earthquake of 1992) would prove embarrassingly more efficient in the delivery of assistance to the destitute than the official agencies charged with these responsibilities. At last, it would become possible for an Islamist-dominated syndicate of lawyers to erect a semipermanent banner at the corner of one of Cairo's busiest intersections on which it was announced for all to see: "Islam Is the Solution."

When the cultural setting of the church shifts, new challenges arise for Christian witness. Such was the case, it seemed to me, for the Protestant (Presbyterian) community that invited us back to Cairo to work again in the Evangelical Theological Seminary. As was the case for Coptic Orthodox Christians, this community likewise had to contend with rising levels of religious violence in the early 1990s, especially in the rural areas of the country south of the capital, whence a majority of our Egyptian seminarians came. Protestant families also had to confront a gnawing sense that opportunities for their children to gain professional and graduate qualifications were constricting year by year. They too heard extremist voices insisting with heightened astringency that Christianity was an alien creed, foreign to Muslim Egypt. And as the century drew to a close, an older generation of Protestants could only reminisce wistfully with fellow believers in the Orthodox tradition about easier days of a more liberal era gone by, when the church was largely left to be itself and neighbors did not regard each other primarily through the lens of religious affiliation.

The difficult circumstances faced by the church in Egypt near the end of the twentieth century have provoked a variety of responses. One option was to leave, and many well-trained Christians have done so, emigrating to the West or to elsewhere in the region where their skills could command high salaries. Others have pulled back into the Christian community by limiting their contact with Muslim neighbors to the greatest extent possible. It was our privilege to live and work with Christian leaders (lay and clergy) who believed passionately that the church's place was in the middle of its society, even when it might not appear to be entirely welcome.

An emblematic event in 1994 brought home to me the tenacity with which Egyptian Christianity has held on to its share of the nation's public space. That year, with the support of several nongovernmental human rights organizations located in the West, an Egyptian NGO, the Ibn Khaldoun Center for Development Studies, had organized an international conference to be held in Cairo on the subject of minorities in the Middle East. Armenians, Berbers, Kurds, southern Sudanese, and Jews outside of Israel were among the groups whose adverse circumstances the participants prepared to discuss. Organizers expected the conference to propose remedies and to advocate for these persecuted minority groups within the *Dar al-Islam*. In the original program, Egypt's Copts were also on the list. It came as something of a surprise then when Pope Shenouda refused to send an official representative to the gathering and raised questions about whether such a conference ought to be held in Egypt at all. Without denying that Christians in Egypt experienced discrimination or that they comprised a demographic minority within their society, Pope Shenouda argued that Christianity had nevertheless to be understood, first of all, as a native phenomenon. Egypt's Christians were not a separate, unassimilated race within a Muslim body politic. Seen from this perspective, the church could claim to be an intrinsic part of Egypt's social fabric, rather than being characterized as some kind of foreign object that had to be tolerated by the majority and protected from without by extraordinary measures.

What I think I heard in this debate was the church renewing its warrant to witness to Jesus Christ in a context it continued to claim as its own. However much their society had been or might be Islamicized, our Protestant colleagues and many other Christian Egyptians had resolved to act on their own specific mandate, the call to be a light to the nations and the Lord's servant in the place God's providence had placed them. New ministries of proclamation were undertaken with tact and creativity, often making use of technology to overcome the restrictions of custom that narrow-mindedness had put in the way. Ministries of service multiplied in the 1990s, pursued at the national level by internationally recognized development organizations such as the Coptic Evangelical Organization for Social Services (CEOSS) and by countless congregations working on a smaller scale in villages, towns, and cities. As had been the case in the history of early Christianity, the power of the church's witness grew in proportion to the hardships faced by the community. More than a few remarkable Egyptian Christians taught me anew what the perseverance of the saints could mean in this life. By implication, their example beggared the nonchalance with which most of us in the West approach the idea of church membership.

By the early 1990s, the Evangelical Theological Seminary had begun to attract a much larger, better qualified, and less uniform student body than had attended when we taught there in the late 1970s. Since then, the total number of students had climbed from about forty to over 160. A majority of those now admitted had already completed an undergraduate degree and many more were women. A lay studies program offered in the evening complemented a morning ordination track schedule. Students attended from many more places in the Arabic-speaking Middle East than had been the case earlier, and a burgeoning contingent of Sudanese, many of them long-term refugees in Cairo, came to comprise nearly one quarter of the student body. Finally, to the main campus in Cairo had been added a branch in Alexandria and an informal study group in the southern city of Assyut.

Within this increasingly diverse student body, I discovered a hunger for theological education. This was evident in the eagerness with which even students preparing for ministry in village settings could take up subjects as culturally arcane for them as New Testament Greek. I saw it in the dedication of the evening students, many of whom came to the campus after a full day's work for several hours of class four nights a week and kept this up for three or more years in a row. That degree, in most cases, would not qualify them to become ordained pastors. Only the desire to become more effective lay leaders motivated them to complete this degree. Out of this group were many individuals already engaged in significant ministries of service and proclamation through their local congregations. Their avidness and energy for the task of Christian witness often humbled my pitiful missionary efforts, but also, at times, inspired and helped me to enlarge my vision of mission.

An invitation to join the faculty at Union Theological Seminary and the Presbyterian School of Christian Education brought this latest excursion among the believers in the *Dar al-Islam* to a close in 1997. This time I carried with me back to the United States two lessons in particular. One was a new understanding of what partnership in mission could mean. Due to the generous spirit of my seminary colleagues in Cairo, I had been given an opportunity to step beyond an observer's role and to function as more than just a technical expert with useful skills to contribute to the cause. Service on the seminary's board of trustees had put me at the heart of the institution's life. Hard work in long committee meetings provided moments to consider together larger matters of purpose and direction, even as the details of everyday life threatened to overwhelm us all. That we came to share a common vision for mission is what made sustained joint action possible and, for me, ultimately meaningful. The foundation of our partnership was not an ideology or a common enemy; it was the conviction that a global church is called to witness in every way possible to the lordship of Jesus Christ.

A second lesson from this most recent stay among the believers is reflected in the language of the previous sentence above. Muslims and Christians in Egypt had taught me the value of explicit affirmations of faith, the importance of demonstrating by word and deed in public what one believes. I returned to the United States grateful, of course, for the rule of law in the West and the individual freedoms and personal safety it guarantees, but the limits of secular diffidence on matters religious in North

Atlantic societies had also been laid bare for me. In the lives of so many dear and courageous Christian friends in Egypt, I had seen examples of forthright witness that could not so easily be dismissed as acts of cultural domination or discounted as the mere outworking of a right-wing political agenda. The facts of demography and context argued otherwise. For their part, Muslims had provided me with a chance to be the object of missionary outreach, sometimes in very direct ways, as ordinary believers shared with me the ground of their faith in God, with an eye toward my conversion to Islam. In the end, what endures is an impression of a society's whole life, richly permeated with religious language and infused with the conviction of faith that yearns to be shared. Participation in this life became an act of liberation for me, an invitation likewise to witness freely. I had learned how to be an evangelical, in what I think is the best and most biblical sense of the word.

Reconciliation

A Vision of Christian Mission

SYNGMAN RHEE

For the love of Christ urges us on, because we are convinced that one has died for all; therefore all have died. And he died for all, so that those who live might live no longer for themselves, but for him who died and was raised for them. . . . So if anyone is in Christ, there is a new creation: everything old has passed away; see, everything has become new! All this is from God, who reconciled us to himself through Christ, and has given us the ministry of reconciliation.
2 Corinthians 5:14–15, 17–18, NRSV

God's reconciliation in Jesus Christ is the ground of the peace, justice, and freedom among nations which all powers of government are called to serve and defend. The Church, in its own life, is called to practice the forgiveness of enemies and to commend to the nations as practical politics the search for cooperation and peace. This search requires that the nations pursue fresh and responsible relations across every line of conflict, even at risk to national security, to reduce areas of strife and to broaden international understanding.
Confession of 1967 (9.45), Presbyterian Church (U.S.A.)

The Roots of Family and Faith

*T*he search for the roots of our faith is a very important task. As I trace my own life in search of those roots, I discover a number of them that have strongly affected my life. Among these varied roots, the deepest ones are those of the faith I received from my grandmother and my parents.

My paternal grandmother was a "Bible woman." The title "Bible woman" was given to the women who taught and nurtured new believers, especially women and children, during the early period of the Korean church's growth. The memories of my grandmother are still very vivid in my mind. When my grandmother first became a Christian in the early 1900s, she faced a great deal of difficulty from my grandfather, who was the head of a rigidly Confucian family, and from other relatives as well. I had heard stories of times when she was not allowed to live in her house after she became a believer and so she had to stay with other Christian families and missionaries for a while. She was a woman of strong faith and she kept her faith despite the harsh pressures she faced. She was a short woman of slender frame who was nonetheless a ball of fire in managing life in such a difficult household. I still hear ringing in my ears the melody and the voice of her joyous hymn singing. My grandparents had two sons, my father and his elder brother. My uncle left North for South Korea soon after Korea's liberation from Japanese rule in 1945, and he later became a minister in the Methodist Church.

My father was a schoolteacher. Under the Japanese occupation of Korea, he joined the movement to fight for the independence of the Korean people. He became classified as a political offender and used to be taken away by high-level police investigators on a regular basis. Even after being released he had to hide in some secluded places. I remember the days he had to be away from home and we missed him very much. It was in this difficult situation that he decided to become a minister.

It was not too long after the liberation of Korea when Korea was divided into North and South and the Democratic Peoples' Republic of Korea (North Korea) was inaugurated with the Communist Party at its center. For the people who struggled for freedom and justice under the Japanese rule, this was yet another ordeal to face. Communism was understood by many as an ideology based on atheism, and therefore, a communist government was an anti-Christian government. Those who had zealously resisted the oppression under the Japanese rule began to challenge the communist system.

Therefore, during the process of establishing the communist regime in North Korea, the political authorities recognized the churches as a major opposition force and considered them to be groups hostile to the regime. Political repression began against the Christians. In an effort to limit the gatherings of Christians and to control the activities of pastors, the Korean Christian Federation was instituted and all pastors were pressured to join the Federation. However, at the beginning, many pastors refused to join the Federation out of their conviction that the newly created communist government should not interfere with the affairs of the church. They lived with fresh memories of their struggle and suffering under the Japanese occupation as they opposed the Shinto shrine worship. Once again, the church leaders faced a test of their faith. Many of them refused and paid the price.

At the time of Korean War in 1950 my father was imprisoned along with other Christian leaders and eventually became a martyr. He was forty-nine years old and I was nineteen. Among many memories of my father, one thing stands out for me: his commitment to ministry even under diffi-cult situations. He kept watch over his church and cared for the members in order to fulfill steadfastly his responsibilities as a pastor right up until the final moment of his life. When the pressure on the church became more intense and my father's coworkers began to leave for the South, many of our relatives urged our family to flee the North as well. As those entreaties increased, my father thought of his church people and said, "As the shep-herd I cannot leave my church members behind and set out to seek only my own survival." He had given up the idea of going to the South.

The entry of United Nations forces into the city of Pyongyang in the autumn of 1950 brought a new life for us. For my family, finding out the whereabouts of our father who had been in prison was the most pressing and urgent concern. At that time many people went to the hills and fields to search for cavities or hollows in the ground so they could dig out the bodies of their loved ones. On the third day of our searching, we discov-ered the body of our father along with those of some fifty other people. As this was a time when so many were unable even to locate the bodies of their loved ones, we were grateful that we at least had found our father's body and could hold his funeral.

My experience as a nineteen-year-old witnessing the funeral of his father became the strong motive behind my new resolve for my life. As I stood before my father's body at the funeral, I cried out to God with grief and anger. In those anguished moments of my life I heard a still small voice saying, "What your father was not able to finish in his life is now what you have to continue." From that moment I have not forgotten that voice from above. The motive for my life lies in that call of God which I heard the day of my father's funeral and to which I have tried to live in faithful response through the years since. After my father's death, my mother decided to send my young brother and me to the South. She believed it was the best way to ensure our safety and survival. The decision was far from an easy one for her or for us. My brother and I fled from Pyongyang on a snowy Sunday morning in December 1950. Since it was a severely cold and very dangerous time, only young and strong men dared to venture on the long walk south. As we traveled to an unknown destiny, we thought of our four sisters, ages fourteen, ten, eight, and four months, and of our mother we left behind. We remembered how our mother had come to the gate of our house, holding our hands and saying, "Pray to God wherever you go, and we shall see each other through our prayers."

We followed long lines of UN troops who were withdrawing from North Korea, pursued by the Chinese communist army. In all, nearly half a million Koreans endured experiences similar to ours as we walked for nearly a month to reach Pusan, near the southern tip of Korea. I remember so vividly how desperate we were on those cold winter days as refugees of the war, not knowing where to go, on a journey of unknown destiny, suffering and destitute, experiencing hunger, thirst, nakedness, and cold. In those days of desperation the love of God touched so many of us through the help of many Christian people, brothers and sisters from the United States.

Church World Service of the National Council of the Churches of Christ in the USA had come with food, drinks, blankets, tents, love, faith, and hope. We were all touched so deeply by that effort. I still remember how grateful I felt to receive that love of God through the help of so many people who had given sacrificially. In such situations, to receive such help is indeed a spiritual experience, going beyond simply the physical goods and services.

Many years later, in 1992, when I was nominated to serve as the president of the National Council of the Churches of Christ in the USA (NCCC), I hesitated quite a bit, asking myself, "Can an immigrant, a foreigner, serve as the president of the NCCC, which represents more than fifty million Christians of thirty-four denominations in this country?" After a time of hesitation I said yes to that challenge, not because I was worthy to be called to that position, but because I was reminded of those days when I received the help to be lifted up from difficult and desperate situations. In grateful response to what the NCCC had done for me and hundreds of thousands of others in those times of need, I said that I would carry on the responsibility in order that the work of Jesus Christ and the church may be carried out this day for people in need and who suffer in so many places around the world.

Soon after coming down to South Korea as refugees, my brother and I joined the South Korean Marine Corps and served for five years during the Korean War. In 1953, I had an opportunity to come to the United States for six months for special training at the U.S. Marine Corps School in Quantico, Virginia. Later, in 1956, with the help from my American Marine friends, I was able to return to America as a student at Davis and Elkins

College in West Virginia. Following my graduation I continued my studies at Louisville Presbyterian Seminary, Yale Divinity School, and Chicago Theological Seminary. I was ordained as a Presbyterian minister in 1960 and served as pastor of Boston Presbyterian Church in Boston, Kentucky, and Westminster Presbyterian Church in Louisville, Kentucky. I later served as a campus minister at the University of Louisville. I often thought of how happy my mother would have been if only she could know that I was following in my father's footsteps as a Christian minister.

Reconciliation and Justice

In the United States, the early part of the 1960s marked a time of intense struggle as African American people engaged in their civil rights struggle. At that time I was a campus minister and teacher at the University of Louisville in Kentucky. I still have fresh memories of how I, as an Asian American minister, joined with black and white Louisville church leaders and with African American university students in support of the movement to pass a public accommodation ordinance in the city of Louisville.

The African American students decided to organize a Black Student Union on the university campus, and according to university regulation they needed to have a faculty advisor. They came to me and asked if I would be willing to serve as their faculty advisor. "Why are you asking me to be your faculty advisor? You know I am not black," I said. "Yes, we know you are not black," they replied, "but we saw you out on the street demonstrating together with us for our civil rights." One student added with a sense of humor, "We know you are not fully baked but you are at least half baked." I felt extremely honored to be asked to be the first faculty advisor for the Black Student Union at the university.

I still remember vividly the frequent occasions when Martin Luther King Jr. came to Louisville and met with us and marched shoulder to shoulder with us on the streets. From the midst of such a difficult life of intense struggles, Dr. King gave us a very precious lesson that has served for me as the foundation of my life's faith and work. This teaching was his conviction that the key to the creation of a new history lies in the hands of the oppressed and suffering people. In the relationship between those who unjustly inflict injury and harm and those who receive those blows, there is a choice of whether to take revenge on those who have done the injustice or instead to form a new relationship for forgiving those persons. The decision rests in the hands of those who have been beaten down, according to Dr. King. He called this truth "vicarious suffering." Dr. King maintained that the civil rights movement was a movement to free not only the oppressed but also for the liberation of the oppressor.

Through my involvement with the civil rights movement, I learned that justice, peace, and love cannot be separated from each other. During one demonstration, a white man asked me why I, an Asian, was involved in the "black and white" issue, as if to say that the civil rights movement was a concern for black and white people alone. My answer was then and is now that human rights is not a black and white issue, or a yellow issue, but a human issue and the church's issue. When the basic rights of any people are trampled down and violated, this is an issue for all of us, not simply for the oppressed.

The Cost of Reconciliation

In 1974 when I was working as Middle East coordinator for the Program Agency of the United Presbyterian Church in the USA, I had an opportunity for a conversation with President Anwar Sadat in Cairo, Egypt. It was a time when feelings of animosity and discord between Israel and the Arab nations were at a high pitch. The pain resulting from the October 1973 war between the Israeli and Egyptian armies had not abated. In spite of this, during the two hours of our conversation at the presidential palace, President Sadat's greatest area of concern focused on the issues and the task of reconciliation and peace.

One particular reason that I respected President Sadat as a great leader was his historical visit to Jerusalem in 1976. He shattered the political situation of impasse that had arisen from years of enmity and the interruption of mutual exchanges by setting out himself for Jerusalem as an emissary of peace. I watched with great interest and was deeply affected by the sight of President Sadat's going to an "enemy land" and riding along its streets. Then the next year as I witnessed Israeli Prime Minister Begin's visit to Cairo and his welcome there, I could not help but think, "Why can't our Korean people do the same?" My heart ached with envy and sadness.

Koreans experienced one war in the early 1950s and they remain as hostile camps even to this day. But the Egyptians and the Israelis were searching for ways that would lead them to peaceful coexistence even after having gone through several wars. I stood in great awe of the decisions and magnanimity of those leaders as they tried to forget the hurts of the past and make every effort to create a new future.

Sadly, however, as President Sadat was carrying out his role as an apostle of peace and reconciliation, he became the victim of assassination by those who opposed his initiatives of reconciliation. I still remember vividly what happened. It was a special day of celebration in Cairo, and as a military parade was passing in front of the platform where the president and other dignitaries were standing, bursts of machine gun fire broke out. President Sadat and many other guests were killed instantly. It was truly an ironic page of history written that day.

Among those killed in that tragedy was one with whom I had worked very closely. He was Bishop Samuel of the Coptic Orthodox Church in Egypt. Responsible for the ecumenical relations of the Coptic Orthodox Church, Bishop Samuel was a church leader of impressive sincerity, ability, and ecumenical vision. He always searched for ways to reconciliation and peace in the midst of very complex and difficult situations of all kinds—between Christians and Jews, between Christians and Muslims, between Orthodox and Protestant churches, and between Israel and Arab nations with their political and ethnic discord. He devoted his whole life to building bridges across many troubled waters. This man's fate became joined with Sadat's as they both paid the price for being peacemakers and reconcilers.

For the Ministry of Reconciliation

In the spring of 1978, an unexpected opportunity arose to bring about the visit home to North Korea I had long dreamed about. The occasion came while I was on a trip in the Middle East. Through a contact with the North Korean embassy in Cairo, there came the invitation to make a visit to North Korea and I had to decide on the spot, without previous planning and without consultations. I was filled with anticipation and anxiety as I boarded a plane for Pyongyang. On my arrival at the government guest house in the capital city, my four sisters were brought to see me for a reunion—after twenty-eight years of separation from each other.

I cannot describe the emotions of love and joy we shared in that reunion. I learned the sad news that my mother had passed away in 1970, eight years before. She had waited twenty years hoping for news about her sons. Our hours together were insufficient for all that we wanted to share with each other, but at least we had the privilege of seeing each other again, a dream that has been denied to countless Koreans who continue to be separated from their loved ones left behind.

Another significant event of my visit was my meeting with Rev. Ryang Wook Kang, then a vice premier of North Korea. I had known Rev. Kang years ago when he was pastor of a Presbyterian church in Pyongyang. He had been a friend of my father and a colleague of my mother in a mission school. In my conversation with Vice Premier Kang I asked about the plight of Christians in North Korea. He told me that there were Christians worshiping in "house churches," since the church buildings had all been destroyed during the war. He was confident that new church buildings would be built later. I was reminded of the truth that seeds of faith planted with the sweat and blood of martyrdom do not die easily.

From among the many reflections on my unexpected trip to North Korea, three main themes emerged. The first was an urgent concern for reuniting the separated families. Korean political and military realities have made it almost impossible for thousands of families who were separated by the war to raise their voices in concern for their loved ones left behind. It has been difficult and risky to seek any information about the separated families in both North and South Korea. An intense longing to know anything about one's family is one of the real, tangible bonds that unite the Korean people. The agony of waiting, of not knowing year after year what happened to those we love, is one of the supreme human tragedies of our time. To do something about such a tragedy is certainly one of the mission tasks of the church.

The second theme was an urgent need for reconciliation in Korea. I have long wondered about the ways we can find to work together to reduce tensions, avoid war, and peacefully resolve the hostilities between North and South. Having gone through war and seen its tragedy, I am convinced that there must never be another war in Korea. Such reflection on the human cost of war will sober anyone who might consider a military solution in Korea. Despite the political estrangement that continues between the two Koreas, there is an increasingly poignant necessity for reconciliation. Deeply broken relationships on the Korean peninsula have caused alienation and estrangement, and these have had a costly effect upon all Korean people. At the same time, every Sunday morning Christians in South Korea, and I dare say in North Korea too, pray fervently for peace and reunification. The power of this desire to again be reunited as one people should not be underestimated. The ministry of reconciliation in places like Korea is also an important mission task of the church.

The third theme was a burning passion to find ways for the gospel to be shared more effectively and for the Christian community to be strengthened. I hold the conviction that the gospel can and must be preached everywhere, including in socialist countries. Yet I am searching for a new form that the Christian community may take in a society like North Korea. Is "churchly" Christianity as we know it viable there? Or must we seek new understandings of how the openness and newness of the gospel may be communicated in the creative tensions that face all Koreans at this moment? This missiological challenge is before the church.

In June 1983 a historic reunion of two Presbyterian churches was celebrated in a moving ceremony held in Atlanta, Georgia. One hundred twenty-three years before, as a result of the Civil War, the Presbyterian Church had been divided into northern and southern branches, and now they were coming together as one church again. I still carry the emotion of that moment of church reunion deep in my heart.

During that reuniting General Assembly another very momentous decision was made. For the first time, the General Assembly took action on behalf of mission to North Korea through the preparation of basic guidelines stating the responsibility of the U.S. churches to help work toward reconciliation for the Korean people. It also stated the church's understanding of the agony of the ten million separated Korean families. It identified the opening of a way for such family members to find each other as a task the church must actively assume from a missional point of view. Among the representatives at the Assembly from the Korean Presbyterian Church in South Korea were some who opposed our church's taking such a position and making such resolutions. Nevertheless, the General Assembly of the Presbyterian Church adopted new guidelines for reconciliation and mission in North Korea.

In 1986 some more specific directions for peace and reunification in Korea were approved by both the General Assembly of the Presbyterian Church (U.S.A.) and the NCCC. As one part of the process of preparing this statement, a ten-member official delegation from the U.S. churches made a visit to both North and South Korea. What a historic event it was!

Although there was some criticism and misunderstanding after those visits, we persevered in making every effort from the standpoint of our faith, with the result that today the majority of church leaders in South Korea acknowledge reconciliation and peaceful reunification of Korea as being indeed a task for the church. As I see with my own eyes their devotion to the promotion of this united movement, I realize once more the deep truth of the biblical promise, "So let us not grow weary in doing what is right, for we will reap at harvest-time, if we do not give up" (Gal. 6:9, NRSV).

At the General Assembly of the Presbyterian Church (U.S.A.) in 1995, delegations of church leaders from South and North Korea met together in Cincinnati, Ohio. It was a historic occasion for them to meet together for the first time officially since the Korean War. Since that time the Presbyterian Church, the United Methodist Church, and other denominations, under the leadership of the NCCC, have expanded the scope of this movement for reconciliation. It will not cease in the future, and I believe firmly that the day will come when the fruits of so much labor will be seen. We still have a long way to go toward a comprehensive reconciliation in Korea, but at the same time we have come a long way. For all of this I can only give God the praise and thanks.

Conclusion

I believe that the gospel of reconciliation is the very core message for the life of Christian faith. It is the story of God's acts of reconciliation toward humanity. I also believe that we are called to follow God by putting the gospel of reconciliation into practice, and that the practice of reconciliation is central to Christian mission. For me personally, reconciliation has become the most valuable cornerstone of my own life of faith.

History teaches us that anyone who accepts the task of working to bring about peace and reconciliation may become a sacrificial victim through whom a new history can be born. The ministry of reconciliation is often costly and difficult. Yet we know the ministry of reconciliation is given to us as we carry out the mission of the church. Beyond this comes the realization that, rather than having stepped forward and taken the cross willingly on our shoulders, almost without our knowing it the cross has been laid there and must be borne. Then we willingly submit to carry that cross as our own and, by God's grace, walk forward step by step.

Toward the Development of a New Christian Missiological Identity

MARSHA SNULLIGAN HANEY

*S*haped by my home congregation, experiences of urban ministry, and cross-cultural experiences of the church on several continents, I understand God as a missionary, liberating God, concerned about all of life. In this essay I will discuss incarnational ministry, contextualization, and identity in light of the Black Church's contribution to the dialogue on Christian mission.

I have the honor and privilege of serving on the theological faculty at my alma mater, Johnson C. Smith Seminary. Johnson C. Smith University (subsequently named Biddle Memorial Institute) was established on April 7, 1867, as part of the Freedmen's College of North Carolina. In 1969 the religion department moved from Charlotte to Atlanta, Georgia, and Johnson C. Smith Theological Seminary (JCSTS) became a part of the consortium of the six Protestant seminaries known as the Interdenominational Theological Center (ITC). The ITC, which is one of the most significant ventures in theological education in America, has as its mission to educate "for the Church and the global community Christian leaders who are committed to and practice a liberating and transforming spirituality, academic discipline, justice and peace, an appreciation of religious, gender and cultural diversity, and a desire to engage the public arena for the common good." While ITC represents the best of the Black Church tradition by bringing together the many resources of the church to address human circumstances (based on the traditional perspective of black ecumenism that is mission-oriented, concerned with the development of the whole person and with liberation, and directed toward securing a position of God-given strength and faithfulness), JCSTS educates from the strengths of what it means to be part of a Reformed, confessional, and connectional church in mission.

As associate professor of missiology and religions of the world, I teach courses in mission theology, mission history, evangelism, and Christian ecumenism, particularly from the perspective of urban theological education. I also teach African and Middle Eastern religions, Christian and Muslim relations, and comparative religions in the African American community, with a focus on learning with others about their faith through pedagogic dialogues and encounters. An example of this is illustrated in a recent trip I made to Cape Town, South Africa. The highlights of the trip included listening to speeches by former South African president Nelson Mandela, Ela Gandhi (granddaughter of Mahatma Gandhi), and the Dalai Lama. I also participated in a Sunrise Peace Pilgrimage to Robben Island, where a peace pole was planted as a symbol of international peace. As I stood on that island, selected because it symbolizes the triumph of the human spirit, I could not help but pray to the One who "is the way and the truth and the life" (John 14:6), and to give thanks for such experiences as this that fuel my passion for Christian mission.

The Incarnational Nature of Mission

I believe Acts 1:8 is as relevant today in our complex and changing world as it was for the original Christian hearers. In this verse the risen Christ says to his disciples, "you will receive power when the Holy Spirit has come upon you; and you will be my witnesses in Jerusalem, in all Judea and Samaria, and to the ends of the earth" (NRSV). I invite readers to revisit this passage with me for several reasons. First, the image of a biblical witness to Jesus beginning in Jerusalem and extending to the "ends of the earth" draws attention to the incarnational nature of Christ. God so loved the world that God shared God's very self with women, men, and children, and invited them into a life-giving relationship through Jesus. The incarnation makes clear God's approach to mission, and through these spoken words, Jesus makes clear how we are to approach mission.

Second, Acts 1:8 provides a significant framework for sharing some of the missional activities I have engaged in, as well as lessons I have learned and taught along the journey. My commitments are to contextualization, pedagogy and interfaith dialogue, and global theological education, particularly in contexts of diversity and complexity where crossing boundaries of difference are not only a social requirement but a theological mandate as well. The structure of this biblical passage allows me to highlight these important concepts of mission.

More importantly, however, Acts 1:8 speaks urgently to the call for integrity, authenticity, and relevance related to the communication of the Christian faith and the "being" of Christian community. Do religious communities have credibility? is not a question we can easily dismiss. Significant changes taking place in the world and within the study of mission compel us to address issues of the integrity of the faithful witness of the church. We now see evidence of a changing context (social and political) of mission, a changing profile of the biblical interpreters, changing interpreters of mission histories, a changing curriculum of mission studies, and a changing mission of theological institutions and mission agencies.

In this challenging era, we must address Christian witness with words, deeds, and lifestyle in the daily contexts in which people work, live, study, build relationships, and seek to live with dignity as human beings. The traditional missiological paradigms no longer suffice. The capacity of Christian education and theological education to develop values (personal, communal, and cultural) to respond to diverse and complex missional challenges is what I am most concerned about. In the new millennium, the global objectives of Christian mission will require Christian leaders who are willing to create a new Christian missiological identity that embraces the diverse witness of the total church and that excludes none.

An influential thinker in my professional development has been church historian Gayraud Wilmore. According to Wilmore, "the challenge of coherency" for missional wholeness requires "the development of a new professional identity as practitioners and strategists of a liberating mission . . . informed by biblical and theological knowledge in dialogue with the human sciences and directed toward the fundamental transformation of persons and institutions of society."[1] In this light, I propose "the challenge of coherency" as a notion critical to the basic formation of a new Christian missiological identity dedicated to inclusion of all of God's people at work in all of life's circumstances. To this vocation of learning, teaching, and enabling faith-based communities (congregations, seminaries, community ministries, and caucuses included) to participate in holistic and authentic Christianity based on a biblical vision, I have devoted my life.

" . . . and you will be my witnesses in Jerusalem . . ."

Whenever I reflect on my own life, as a seventh generation African American, and how God has acted in circumstances, events, and through persons to prepare me to participate in the life and mission of the church, I am truly and deeply humbled. I do not know when I first sensed the presence of God in my life, but I grew up knowing that I was loved. My parents, Jesse B. Snulligan and the late Princess Murray Snulligan, taught me and my two sisters, through words and example, the importance of family, prayer, church, and community.

When a young pastor (also a graduate of JCSTS), new to the city of St. Louis, went from house to house inviting members of our neighborhood to consider belonging to a newly forming congregation in 1956, my father responded positively. Rev. Dr. William Gillespie, this founding pastor, has provided continuous leadership to the Cote Brilliante Presbyterian Church to this day. What began as a commitment to a vision of ministry in the midst of white flight in a changing neighborhood has grown to become the largest African American Presbyterian church in the denomination, with an effective Christian influence throughout the city. I attribute this to the leadership of Dr. Gillespie, who recognized the need to prepare the congregation for great leadership in the future. He worked hard to inspire people, especially through preaching and personal compassion, to reach out to others, and to grapple with life's issues through both personal faith and the experience of what it means to be the *ecclesia* in the midst of change.

According to biblical history, the city of Jerusalem was very much like any other ordinary city. It was not without troubles. People lived, planted gardens, built water supplies and streets, houses and temples, as well as burial grounds. However, what made Jerusalem so important was the belief that it was the chosen city of the one true God, a city with a mission to reveal God to the world.

In linking my personal story to God's story, my family and home church represent "my Jerusalem," the place where I first witnessed Christian faith, learned of the triune God, and discovered what it meant to live as a person of faith, concerned for God and others.[2] These were lessons learned from the perspective of both the Black Church heritage and the Presbyterian tradition. Cote Brilliante Presbyterian Church, in its priestly role, taught me that the incarnation of God is revealed not primarily in ideas, but in concrete realities and relationships. God's Holy Spirit, I learned, was not only present during my baptism, confirmation, and participation in the Lord's Supper, but God's revelation was also made real in the nurture, guidance, and kindness of church members. As a young person, I cherished the affirmation our church gave to youth ministry, even in the face of other congregational and budgetary priorities.

Concerning the prophetic role of the church, my pastor and congregation were there to provide spiritual and social guidance when racial violence erupted as a result of the integration of myself and twenty-six other African Americans into a high school of two thousand white students. In the pastoral role, when my mother died prematurely, leaving my father to raise three daughters (one in seminary, one in college, and one in high school), our home congregation continued to be a source of strength and compassion. Today, even though my father and stepmother have moved to the suburbs, they continue to make the half-hour journey to Cote Brilliante to worship.

Although I have ministered with congregations in Detroit, Atlanta, Cleveland, Pasadena, and Los Angeles in various capacities during my twenty-two years as an ordained Presbyterian minister, I will always be grateful for the lessons in theological faithfulness experienced in that healthy congregation. Undergirded by a solid theological education at JCSTS, I experienced within this congregation a deeper understanding of the role of the local church in the overall life and vitality of Christian mission. Mission, I have discovered, is done best by those who are most fully involved in the life of society and who can reflect theologically. As research on congregations has indicated, congregations are important because they are gathering places for people to learn to trust and belong. As congregations replace the traditional family by serving in the role of extended family, many new opportunities are available for incarnational mission.

" . . . and in all Judea . . ."

While there is no denying the social diversity (ethnic, gender, racial, class, and age) represented in the image of Jerusalem, the image of Judea alludes to even greater social diversity and more cultural differences. Just as the land of Judea described in scripture indicated a wider extension into the whole country of the Canaanites, "my Judea" consisted of opportunities that have enabled me to gain insight into the challenges and obstacles created as a result of living in a multicultural and multiethnic society. The social boundaries and theological differences found within a context of a common faith and culture can be a challenge to bridge.

Two experiences brought home to me the challenge of diversity within a common community. The first was a unique opportunity provided by San Francisco Theological Seminary's extension program for Professor Warren Lee and myself to teach a course entitled, "Ministry in a Multicultural Setting" in Los Angeles. In the midst of teaching that course, the Rodney King event occurred with his infamous question, "Why can't we all get along?" The violence and its aftermath provided a unique opportunity for our diverse class to reflect on the meaning of ministry in diverse contexts, prompting new social awareness and sense of the importance of congregational life in community.

The second illustration of the challenge of diversity within a shared religious heritage occurred in 1982 when I was commissioned by The United Presbyterian Church in the U.S.A. to serve as a missionary to the Presbyterian Church in the U.S. I was to serve in the Division of International Ministries, Office of Personnel Recruitment, as Racial-Ethnic Recruiter for Overseas Opportunities. This involved traveling to different parts of the country to engage in mission education, advocacy, and training among African American, Asian American, Hispanic American, and Native American congregations and caucuses. This was a watershed event because it allowed me to see how other ethnic groups sought to address their issues of culture, religion, and society. It also served to strengthen my resolve to engage in what has been termed "spiritlinking," whereby one broadens one's circle of friends and relationships to achieve new life in an organization that is resistant to transformation or change.[3]

Within this ministry, my tasks entailed helping the church to formulate and manage mission policies, as well as raise awareness related to issues of mission leadership development, education, and recruitment among persons labeled as racial ethnic within the denomination. When I think about Presbyterian identity and mission from the perspective of our national church with its current challenges of ethnic diversity, I think of G. Thompson Brown's brief but significant article entitled, "Presbyterian Identity and Mission." In it, he suggests that the "identity crisis" of the Presbyterian Church at times during our history has been corrected and transformed by our sense of mission.

This article (in *The Presbyterian Outlook*, April 8, 1996) declares, "[In 1861, southern Presbyterians created] two statements which they wished to hold up before the world as defining their identity as a newly organized church. The first was a theological statement which today we would rather forget. It was a defense of the institution of slavery based on scriptural grounds. The second was a missiological statement which gave a ringing call and commitment to the worldwide mission of the church of Jesus Christ." Three critical issues that Brown highlights—race/ethnicity, theology, and missiology—remain a concern for the church today and must be addressed if we are to have integrity within a diverse society.

The first issue concerns the social construct of race. Racism and white ideology cannot be ignored, especially if our denomination is to achieve any portion of the 2020 churchwide strategy goals related to racial ethnic evangelism and church growth. Even as this essay is being prepared, some social scientists, such as Carl Rowan and Andrew Hacker, suggest that our society is on the brink of a race war. I have some understanding of how ambiguously Christian theology has been communicated in relation to the issue of race/ethnicity. This ambiguity has, in part, resulted in unprecedented religious pluralism within the African American community. In my book *Islam and Protestant African American Churches: Responses and Challenges to Religious Pluralism,* I contend there is more openness to Islam among those who have had negative experiences in the church or where Christianity failed to adequately address issues such as race and racism. Various genetic, biological, anthropological, sociological, and psychological theories (such as the "Bell Curve") have been and continue to be used to support prejudices against African Americans and the theological and ecclesiastical structures that sustain them. This social construction of race continues to haunt the church, and many ITC seminarians have had to address it as a crucial missional concern.

The second issue of concern the article raises is that of theology. Theology does matter. We must be as willing in contemporary society as other faith communities (including Baha'i, Buddhist, Muslim, and Southern Baptist) to articulate and live a holistic theology that addresses the dignity of every human being from a Reformed perspective. The church's credibility has been weakened by popular Reformed Protestant and Catholic theologies that have given rise to and perpetuated, among other things, the enslavement of African men, women, and children for economic gain, the doctrine of the elect (presenting itself anew in the Christian Identity movement), the myth of Ham and the "divine curse," and apartheid. As a result of the damage done by these theologies, Christian education and theological education have had to include theological deconstruction and reconstruction as part of their missional outreach concerns.

Finally, it must be acknowledged that while the classic notion of missiology consisted of an affirmation of the principles of self-government, self-propagation, and self-support overseas, the principle of self-theologizing (referred to as contextual theology) has not been so widely promoted and nurtured, either within the United States or abroad. It is only in recent decades that the theological voices of those once marginalized from missiology and missiological dialogues are now being articulated and framed afresh. Ethnic studies and contextual theologies, as well as colonial and postcolonial missional studies, reveal not only new biblical hermeneutics, but also new Christian theologies and a variety of ways of doing theology. I witnessed how important this process is recently as I taught and learned with theological graduate students in Salatiga, Indonesia.

From my perspective, this is a welcome reality for two reasons. First, it has demonstrated the importance of mutuality in mission and the necessity for appropriate partners in mission. Second, it has served to highlight how important missiology is, not only in the life of Christians but for the faithful of other living religions as well who are seeking to utilize their spiritual resources in addressing problems related to life's disconnections. Last year I attended a Muslim-Christian seminar at the University of Legion in Accra, Ghana, and listened attentively to Imam Elijah Suleman. He made the following observation: "We [African Muslims] say they [African Americans] left Africa with the Qur'an, they endured with the Qur'an, they persevered with the Qur'an, and they are now returning with the Quran." Theology and missiology are two sides of the same coin, and it is only as we are able to think and act holistically as the global church that we will be able to address with biblical faithfulness challenges such as religious diversity. Only as we posture ourselves for transformational mission will we be able to affirm the interconnectedness of the triune God, as well as the gospel's mandate to live together as the body of Christ.

In the midst of my Judean experiences, which are frequently marred by the lack of a sense of mutuality in mission across racial ethnic lines, I have learned to cherish the missional colleagues who understand the need for an appropriate response. Today I am most encouraged by two recent encounters. At the 1999 meeting of the American Academy of Religion, I presented a paper in the Womanist Approaches to Religion and Society section that was well received, indicative of a new level of interest in interreligious dialogue. I also volunteer at the Open Door Ministry in Atlanta, where an awesome practical, holistic ministry among homeless persons and prisoners exists. These examples remind us that transformational mission will only occur as the church interdependently deals with change holistically by analyzing theological and social structures, forms, and meanings that go beyond the symptoms. Often I have discovered that crossing social boundaries and theological differences that motivate, form, and direct our relationships with one another within the same culture (with a common language, but with different ethnic, cultural, regional, and historic memories and worldviews) can be even more challenging to bridge than relationships involving a different language, culture, society, histories, worldviews, and great geographical boundaries.

" . . . and Samaria . . ."

While the boundaries of Samaria in the time of Christ are difficult to determine, biblical history does record the animosity between the Samaritans and the Jews. Endeared to their own religious worldview, sacred beliefs, places, memories, myths, and rituals, the Samaritans considered their religious faith superior to that of the Jews. Feelings of superiority ran just as deep with the Jews, as we see reflected in the story of Jesus and the Samaritan woman. Mission in Samaria is mission among those of very different, even hostile, backgrounds.

The Samaria experiences that have most influenced my understanding of missiology as ecumenical and interfaith witness have been those of living, learning, and engaging in Christian ministry overseas, especially in Birmingham, England; Juba, Sudan; and Kumba, Cameroon. These experiences began when I left my fiance in Atlanta to fulfill a commitment I had made to serve in Sudan following the completion of seminary. In order to prepare to work with the Sudan Council of Churches in Juba, I engaged in Islamic studies at the Selly Oak Colleges in Birmingham. While there I had the opportunity to learn and share with Muslim scholar Askari Hassan, Islamist David Kerr, German theologian Roswith Gerloff, Jamaican theologian George Mulrain, and Bishop Lesslie Newbigin, but the richest lessons were learned from the many ordinary Africans and Palestinians who were living there as the result of dislocation in their home countries.

In Birmingham I discovered the enthusiasm and faithfulness of the Church of the Cherubim and Seraphim, my first worship encounter with non-Western Christianity. I also had my first encounter with globalization as represented by various manifestations of cultural, mental, physical, social, and spiritual violence inflicted around the world. While this was a very good first cross-cultural experience, it was a shocking and painful way to first encounter the profound problems confronting the world church.

In 1979 in Sudan, I was introduced to religious pluralism through the encounter of Islamic, ethnic, and national violence. I experienced among the Christian Sudanese a depth of spirituality that I had never encountered before. It continued to offer hope, grace, and mercy to women, men, and children in the face of death, famine, poverty, violence, and dignity-denying forces. Because the Sudanese government required all students to study a religion, I taught Christian education in a government high school and assisted the Ministry of Religious Education in developing a unified religious education curriculum for the entire nation. I also assisted with the women's ministry program. The Sudanese who first told me about his home country when we were classmates at JCSTS, Rev. Ezekiel Kutjok, continues to be my mentor even as he faithfully serves the Presbyterian Church in Sudan, with some of my PC(USA) colleagues alongside of him. He continues to challenge me with his neverending question: Have our sisters and brothers in America forgotten us as we continue to struggle in war?

I returned from Sudan and married my fiance. In 1984 my husband and I were both commissioned as mission workers, this time with the Presbyterian Church in Cameroon. I went to serve as a pastor and chaplain related to the synod's ministry of evangelism, and my husband served as a high school science teacher and youth leader. I struggled with cultural issues, such as offering the communion cup to both wives of one husband but denying it to the husband (yet accepting his tithes and offerings!). I learned, however, to respect not only African traditional religion but also the church as it wrestled with issues of religion and culture. I often reflect on a question I was once asked related to religious plurality: "If you think you are a good Christian [or Muslim, or Rastafarian, etc.], what sacrifices are you willing to make in the name of that religion?" The three years I spent in Cameroon were defining years for claiming my missiological vocation, and it was there that I decided to earn my master's and doctoral degrees in missiology and intercultural studies from Fuller Theological Seminary in Pasadena, California.

" . . . and to the ends of the earth"

According to biblical historians, in the first century, biblical Ethiopia (which included present-day Sudan) constituted the uttermost southern part of the known world, which then only included the outer reaches of the Roman Empire. I have traveled to Ethiopia with Dr. David Wallace, dean of JCSTS, and others to encounter the Ethiopian Tewahedo Church, a Christian communion that traces its origins to the Old Testament. My experience of Ethiopia was as a leader of a seminar sponsored by the All Africa Conferences of Churches and the Religious Heritage of the African World, a research action-advocacy project of ITC, one in which our denomination has supported student involvement. For me, the significance of Acts 1:8 does not lie in any particular geographical representation, but rather in the challenge of faith communities to link local and global manifestations of authentic Christian faith and witness during times of great social change.

In this spirit, not one of theological tourism, I encourage students at JCSTS to participate in missional activities (within their local communities as well as with the Bossey Institute and the Presbyterian's United Nations Seminar), and they do. I participate in the World Alliance of Reformed Churches (as a member of the Reformed and Pentecostal Dialogue), on a research team studying theological education in Muslim contexts with the Centre for the Study of Non-Western Christianity at

Edinburgh University, and in other denominational groups and activities. Experiences such as these allow me to broaden my curriculum offerings, resources, and partnerships so that students also are challenged by what I see and experience.

The ability of the church, in all its diversity, to have a collective witness and impact on the complex and interrelated issues facing us in this post-modern period will be the result of recognizing our common call to mission and ministry. As we listen to the theologically lived stories of women, men, and children within and concerning their own Jerusalem, Judea, Samaria, and end-of-the-earth types of encounters of the Christian faith, we cannot help but be reminded that the world belongs to God, the church belongs to Jesus and that it is the Spirit who will guide us in all truth. People know how the Spirit has been working in their lives, in ways that you and I have no way of knowing. The recent challenge is described best by Robert Schreiter in the notion of "the glocal" as the new context for theology, where local cultures encounter and negotiate their relationship to the global context.[4] Our ability to respond faithfully to the new missional realities in the twenty-first century depends largely upon our collective efforts to confront hopelessness and anomie, violent conflicts, economic disparity and poverty, health crises, and racial, cultural, and ethnic discrimination. Such an approach has the potential of communicating Christian mission and evangelism as processes of restorative spirit, strengthened by spiritual awareness, faith, and praxis.

Toward the Development of a New Missiological Identity

Where do I think mission is headed? Those who are concerned about mission studies and the praxis of mission must consider the need for the development of a new missiological identity. It must be one that truly respects the diversity of God's mission and that recognizes the desire of witnesses in every context to follow Jesus in a diverse and often painful world where women, men, and children seek human affirmation and meaning.

We can find many models of what it means to be a missional community as we explore the meaning of faith within complex relationships, structures, and systems toward human transformation. The idea of the pilgrim model, in which we all recognize that we journey together, combined with human archaeology as a form of inquiry, seems most appropriate to me.[5] Such a model not only identifies the need for a holistic and integral understanding of Christian mission, it also identifies the need for ethics (an ethic of risk, an ethic of responsibility, and a willingness to affirm plurality) as necessary for theological inquiry. More importantly, the pilgrim model I am suggesting serves to remind us that it is God who is the creator of the mission of the church and not ourselves. Only then can our pains, frustrations, and fears become avenues for courageous and creative faithfulness across boundaries of difference.

A question raised at the 1999 BiNational Service Week of Work provides an example of how we might start on a journey toward a new missiological identity through the engagement of a living dialogue. This question was raised in relation to the theme of identity, and concerns how the North Atlantic church seeks faithfulness in mission: How can a church deal with the hopes and pains of its ethnic communities without capitulating to the pressure of their ethnic aspirations and thereby losing its own identity as a church? This is a valid concern, especially for churches not postured with the same history of dominance, privilege, and hegemony. Equally valid are the questions articulated in marginalized ethnic and postcolonial faith-based communities:

1. Do the organizational patterns, management styles, and strategies of contemporary mission reflect the lessons learned from enslavement, segregation, and colonial and postcolonial experiences?
2. How are the visions, aspirations, and strategies of a nation in which 54 percent of the people define themselves as African American, Asian American, Hispanic/Latino American, American Indian, Middle Eastern American, or blended best represented in the Presbyterian Church (U.S.A.) with its 94 percent Caucasian membership?
3. Are the church's local and global scopes, its networks and partnerships, and the necessity for fostering new ways of "being" (as the accumulation of knowing and doing) in mission adequately reflected in managerial decisions about mission engagement?
4. Are our church and missional organizations, ministries, caucuses, and committees taking adequate account of the upsurge of local church participation and engagement in local communities and congregations?
5. How can ethnic churches in North America deal with the hopes and pains of local communities (religious, economic, and political) within which they live, work, and have their being without capitulating to the pressure of Eurocentric ethnic aspirations and thereby losing their own identity as authentic and relevant?

In other words, are we able to engage in an identity transformation that will allow us to explore the complex interrelationships and tensions (theological and anthropological) that exist between and among us? Furthermore, are we able to embrace as critically thinking missiologists the diverse interpretations of being Presbyterian with an emphasis on the incarnational nature of God's mission and Jesus' requirement for faithful witness throughout the world?

What follows are steps indicating how the traditional, convenient, and familiar patterns of mission defined by paternalism, exclusion, and elitism might give way to a new paradigm of mission leadership. This paradigm identifies our common call for response to the *missio Dei* from the *ecclesia* of every nation, language, and people group.

1. While the Christian truth is not relative, we need to recognize human perspectives on truth are relative, subjective, and limited. Christianity teaches that we must embrace a critical approach that affirms that only God has all truth and that, due to human finiteness, "we only see dimly" (1 Cor. 13:12).

2. The focus of mission must be reconsidered and centered on ways of being (postures) rather than only on ways of doing (processes). In Luke 4:18–19, Jesus is not only the means of salvation, but he also provides the model for the church's posturing itself (incarnationally) within the world.

3. Holistic understandings of Christian mission as God's creation and "missions" as our response to God's mission must be the result of shared reflections on the Word, by the Spirit, and in community.

4. Congregations and other faith communities must embrace an understanding of being in the context of relationship; not only relationship with God, but also relationship with one another, and with all of God's creation.

5. Incarnational ministry begins by engaging in a respectful relationship with people, in a context that honors God, and with the self-defining Jesus Christ as experienced in the biblical witness and in the daily experiences of ordinary life.

6. By affirming diversity (the humanity of those we experience as "other") and engaging and appreciating all gifts, we enrich the body of Christ and the world God so loved.

I raise these issues to stimulate new thinking on missions and why we urgently need a new missiological identity. It must be one that not only tolerates but welcomes people from east and west, north and south, people who already sit at God's table and are ready, able, and willing to think responsibly and critically about God's call to engage in God's mission through Jesus Christ. This new identity will enable the entire church to "Go now, and serve the Lord."

NOTES

1. Gayrand S. Wilmore, ed., *African American Religious Studies: An Interdisciplinary Anthology* (Durham, N.C.: Duke University Press, 1989), 357.

2. The significance of linking our story with God's story is discussed by Anne Streaty Wimberly in *Soul Stories: African American Christian Education* (Nashville: Abingdon, 1994).

3. Spiritlinking is defined as "the deliberated and untiring act of working through resistance to organizational transformation by building the circle of friends, fostering networks of human compassion and interweaving teams of relationships through which new ideas are born and new ways of responding to the mission find expression" (Donna J. Markham, *Spiritlinking Leadership: Working through Resistance to Organization Change* [Mahwah, N.J.: Paulist Press, 1995], 5).

4. See *Theological Education, the Journal of the Association of Theological Schools* with introduction by Robert J. Schreiter, S.J., 35, no. 2 (Spring 1999): 8.

5. See Katie Geneva Cannon's book, *Katie's Canon: Womanism and the Soul of the Black Community* (New York: Continuum, 1995) for a description of human archaeology as a form of theological inquiry. For a description of the pilgrim model, see Jim Plueddermann's article, "SIM's Agenda for a Gracious Revolution," in the *International Bulletin of Missionary Research* 23, no. 4 (1999): 156.

Unfinished Journey

My Pilgrimage in Mission

PHILIP L. WICKERI

> *We shall not cease from exploration*
> *And the end of all our exploring*
> *Will be to arrive where we started*
> *And know the place for the first time.*[1]

*H*istory is our biography, and theology is a reflection of biography, at least in part, especially for a journey in mission, where particular people, places, and issues play an especially important role in shaping our faith and experiences. It is very dangerous to speak of God's purpose in all of this, but we may be able to discern a sense of our calling if we can learn to look backward and forward at the same time.

I grew up in the town of Pelham, outside New York City, and was raised a Presbyterian in Huguenot Memorial Church. We were Presbyterians because that was the closest and most convenient church in this upwardly mobile community. Huguenot was an active, liberal church, committed to mission. We had a series of distinguished pastors, including George Sweazy, who became the professor of evangelism at Princeton the very year I entered seminary, and Bill Schram, who led our church into greater social involvement. I remember listening to missionaries whom we supported in Korea teaching us about what it meant to be a world church. I also remember how the elders of the church were shocked when Bill Schram became involved in the civil rights movement. But when Mickey Schwerner, a graduate of our high school, was murdered in 1964 in Philadelphia, Mississippi, together with Andrew Goodman and James Chaney, many in our youth group felt that Mickey's death had challenged the faith and values of our community.

Colgate

At Colgate University, I became involved in the student antiwar movement and increasingly felt that the church did not speak to our concerns in any meaningful way. Yet I chose to be a philosophy and religion major because I still had so many unanswered questions. I took courses on Kierkegaard, Tillich, and Eastern religions, taught by Kenneth Morgan, who served as my advisor. Tillich had a way of speaking to our situation without demanding anything in the way of commitment to the church. My study of Buddhism and Hinduism introduced me to a whole new world of religious life where the church was also conveniently absent.

The student movement became increasingly radical in the late 1960s and divorced from our university studies. When I joined the students who took over the administration building at Colgate in 1968, most of the professors opposed us. By this time, we had given up on "their" kind of liberalism, believing that it was tainted by its association with the political establishment. We read Marx, Mao, and Marcuse, and were inspired by what was happening with students all over the world—in Paris and Mexico City, at Columbia, Cornell, and Berkeley, and in China and the Cultural Revolution. My interest in Asia increasingly focused on China, which in some way brought the religious and political strands of my life together, although I had only a vague sense of how this was so. I was experiencing a divorce between the personal and the political as my faith became more inward, barely Christian, and my politics became more radical. I took classes and planned demonstrations by day, and deep into the night I continued to read Zen Buddhism and the existentialists. Music and riotous living helped, and, although "I didn't inhale," I believed with many others that we were, as Thomas Wolfe expressed it, "young and drunk and twenty, and we would never die."

In 1968, I attended a student conference at New York University. The speaker had been a missionary in Latin America, and although I did not want to have anything to do with missionaries, I went to hear him. He spoke about the need to combine the faith of the church with radical involvement in society in a way I had never heard before. That speech by Richard Shaull changed my life. I began to reconnect with the faith I had grown up with, something that didn't happen very often in the 1960s, and I decided to go to seminary. Bill Schram urged me to consider Union, his alma mater, as did several of my college professors. But my choice was Princeton, where Dick Shaull was teaching, and during my visit there, I discovered that there were many others also interested in the international mission of the church.

The summer after I graduated from Colgate, I attended Chinese language school at Middlebury College. I was still not sure what I would do with the language, but the teachers—most of whom were in the Chinese department at Princeton University—urged me to continue. It was at Middlebury that I met Janice Kay Latourelle, also a student of Chinese, on her way to spend her senior year at Princeton University. We were married the following year, and Janice has been part of my journey throughout these thirty years. She will not appear very much in the reflections that follow, for she has an unfinished journey of her own.

Princeton

When I arrived on the campus of Princeton Theological Seminary in September 1969, students were already deeply involved in the antiwar movement and in efforts to call the church to a greater sense of social accountability. In the Presbyterian Church, we believed that the Confession of 1967 had given us a new mandate, as did the papers that came out of the 1966 Conference on Church and Society and the Uppsala Assembly of the World Council of Churches.

But seminary was much more for me than the reaffirmation of "the movement" on theological grounds. At Princeton, I was introduced to the writings of Karl Barth, and these challenged my easy theological compromises with the student world. I came at Barth through courses in mission and ethics taught by Charles West. I also read Bonhoeffer, the Niebuhrs, and Paul Lehmann, and found their approach to issues of church and society compelling. This Christocentric attack on liberal culture called me personally to account, and pushed me to come to terms with who I was and where I stood as a Christian.

Dick Shaull had long since ceased to think of himself as a Barthian, but the radicality of Barth's challenge still shaped his approach to social issues. Dick's classes were filled with both North American and international students, and his vision was inspiring. He spoke about "the end of the road and a new beginning" in societies characterized by rapid social change. Still influenced by Paul Lehmann's *koinoinia* ethic, he also emphasized the need to establish "beach heads of a new order" based on a new vision of the *oikumene.* He always pushed us to see beyond the horizon, instilling in us a lifelong orientation toward personal and social change in light of the Christian promise.

The work of Eugene Rosenstock-Huessy became especially important for me. He was a theological polymath oriented toward history who had set out to show that society in the West had very literally come out of revolution. It was he who said that history is autobiography given meaning by Christian faith. Rosenstock-Huessy wrote that the motto of our times should be neither Anselm's *credo ut intelligam*, nor Descartes' *cogito ergo sum*; rather our motto should be *respondeo etsi mutabor*, "I respond though I will be changed," for truth is living and must be socially represented.[2] I did not know it then, but this simple motto may be used to describe the way in which I have tried to respond to new challenges in mission, especially after I went to China.

The challenges I experienced during these years at Princeton came not only from professors and books, but from fellow students and international lecturers. Paulo Friere and Rubem Alves spoke to us, both of whom had been colleagues of Dick Shaull in Brazil. My interest in Asia continued, but for the first time I came into contact with Asian Christians. The Sri Lankan evangelist D. T. Niles spoke in one of our classes, and he helped me to see that Christianity could no longer be regarded as a Western faith. Among the Asian Christians whom I got to know at Princeton were Yong-Bock Kim, Feliciano Carino, K. C. Abraham, Preman Niles, Hilario Gomez, Masahiko Sawa, Nantwan Boonprasat, and Charles Amjad-Ali. Except for Preman Niles who was in Old Testament, they were all doctoral students working with Shaull and West (and later Gibson Winter), and they all became outstanding theologians and ecumenical leaders, as well as lifetime friends and colleagues.

Tainan

My interest in Chinese led me to Margaret Flory, who worked in a variety of mission capacities for the Presbyterian Church at 475 Riverside Drive in New York. Margaret has a wonderful way of bringing people together around the issues that concern them most. She is also a forceful person, to whom it was difficult to say no, and most of us never did. I had spoken with her about the possibility of an internship in Asia, but I was unprepared for her enthusiastic phone call halfway through my second year at Princeton. "Phil," she said, "I am so excited. You and Janice are going to Tainan, Taiwan in September." And of course we went.

Before we left, I managed to pick up a copy of Roland Allen's *Missionary Methods, St. Paul's or Ours?* Allen had been a missionary in China at the turn of the century, and Charles West, another China missionary, suggested that I read him. Roland Allen was sharply critical of the Western missionary movement, and has been called "the great theologian of oncoming decolonization." He spoke of the need for reliance on the work of the Holy Spirit who initiates mission, and emphasized the importance of self-government, self-support, and self-propagation in what were then called the "younger" churches. He is also an important bridge figure in mission, and has attracted the attention of Catholics and Protestants, evangelicals and Pentecostals. Roland Allen is the only missiologist from the first part of the last century who is still relevant in our own.[3]

Tainan in the early 1970s was a very livable city, with many cultural sites, and without the traffic congestion and pollution that plagues the entire island today. We were given a small apartment at the historic Tainan Theological Seminary, where we taught English. We also taught at Cheng Kung University, helped out at the university's Christian Student Center, and continued our study of Chinese. Everyone we met in Tainan was very welcoming, and this became our initial experience of the importance of hospitality both in Christian mission and in Chinese culture.

The Presbyterian Church in Taiwan was the largest Taiwanese organization on the island and a leading voice for Taiwanese aspirations since the late nineteenth century. By the early 1970s, however, there was considerable tension between the Presbyterian Church and the government, exacerbated by the publication of several statements by the Presbyterians about "self-determination" for the people of Taiwan. In light of the growing rapprochement between the United States and mainland China, Taiwanese Christians were speaking prophetically for their people, and Tainan Theological Seminary had become an important center for theological efforts in support of self-determination.

Janice and I did not understand the significance of this at the time. We were trying to learn what it meant to be in mission as young Americans who did not want to be neocolonialists or missionary imperialists. Like so many mission volunteers before us, we said that we had come to learn, and that we would adapt ourselves to the environment in which we were living. I took courses on neo-Confucianism at Cheng Kung University, but I also became interested in Taiwanese literature and considered it an honor when I was asked to purchase the first books on this subject for the seminary library. This was part of the contextualization process, and I discovered that Taiwanese culture was expressed in everything from the food we ate to the folk religious celebrations at nearby temples.

I did not want to impose anything on my students or colleagues, but of course I was unaware of the cultural baggage that I brought along with me. Dan Beeby and other missionary colleagues were patient with me, despite my continuing questions about the whole enterprise in which we were involved. Ch'ing-fen Hsiao, a Princeton Seminary graduate who became principal of Tainan Seminary when I was there, and other seminary colleagues kept pressing me to see the importance of something more than just learning in Christian mission, and through them I developed a new understanding of the church.

My main commitments had been to the student movement and to the new forms of community that it generated. William Thompson, the stated clerk of the United Presbyterian Church, had said that the Christian needed to be converted to Christ, to the church, and to the world. But for me, conversion to the church came last, and it came in Asia. Until then, I had been a sharp critic of what I saw as a compromised institution. In Taiwan, I learned the importance of what it means to be the church in a minority situation. Until I became immersed in the life of the church in Asia; until I experienced the many ways in which Asian churches ministered to me, a stranger from a foreign land; and until I saw how fragile and imperfect Asian churches stood by their people in what at times were extraordinarily difficult situations, I had no idea what the church was all about. The church became one of the many gifts that Asia gave to me.

When I returned to Princeton for my last year of M. Div. studies, most of the students I had known earlier had already graduated. I spent most of my time studying and trying to find a way for Janice and me to return to Taiwan after graduation. I had decided not to seek ordination because I wanted to pursue lay ministry in Asia, and I believed that ordination would link me too much to older forms of missionary practice. Many friends and family members kept asking when we would settle down, but slowly we came to see that this was not really our question.

My M. Div. thesis at Princeton focused on Christianity in the nineteenth-century Taiping revolutionary movement in China. Through this study, I became increasingly interested in the development of contextual Christianity in non-Western societies and in Christian movements that were related to the missionary movement, even as they challenged it. I was awarded the prize in church history for this work, and this allowed me time for more travel and research. We returned to Tainan and lived outside the seminary compound, while teaching and continuing our research. We lived in Taiwan for another two years (1974–1976), and my sense of calling seemed to be deepening.

Princeton Again, Then Hong Kong

When I began doctoral studies at Princeton in 1976, I knew that I wanted to work on Christianity and social movements, with a dissertation focused on China, but I had no clear idea for a dissertation topic. I was interested in how Christian faith moved people to participate in social change, and believed that this could best be understood historically rather than in the world of ideas, theological or otherwise.

China was always on the horizon during the late 1970s. Church representatives had begun to visit China, and they came back with reports of conversations with Christian leaders such as K. H. Ting and Zhao Fusan. I began working on a part-time basis with Franklin Woo, director of the China Program at the National Council of Churches during this time. He and his wife Jean had been Presbyterian missionaries in Hong Kong for many years, and Frank helped me to see ways in which Christians from overseas could become involved in China without repeating the mistakes of colonial times.

In the late 1970s, as interest in China was growing in the churches, the Presbyterians appointed me to be a mission coworker in order to follow events on their behalf in Hong Kong. I had been a Volunteer-in-Mission, an Overseas Associate, a Binational Servant, and now a mission coworker, thus completing the cycle of Presbyterian mission appointments. It was clear that I was not to be a missionary to China in any sort of conventional way, but it was not exactly clear what I would be. Newton Thurber, who was then East Asia liaison for the Program Agency, was a strong advocate of the ecumenical approach to mission and relationships. He helped me to decide to accept and shape the appointment, and he continued to urge me to follow new approaches in relationship to China, and to go where the Spirit led.

Shortly before leaving for Hong Kong, we received word that China was sending a delegation to take part in the Third World Conference on Religion and Peace in Princeton. I was asked to serve as an interpreter and liaison together with Don MacInnis, who had done pioneering work in following religious developments in China. The delegation was headed by Zhao Puchu, president of the Chinese Buddhist Association, and included four prominent Chinese Protestant leaders: K. H. Ting, Han Wenzao, Chen Zemin, and Li Shoubao, as well as Buddhists and Muslims. I learned a great deal from my time with the entire delegation, and the idea for my doctoral dissertation emerged out of their approach to "seeking the common ground, while reserving differences," which they pursued at the conference.

I was commissioned as mission coworker at the meeting of the Program Agency in Sacramento, after which we flew to Hong Kong, with our eighteen-month-old daughter Elisabeth in tow. In Hong Kong, I was assigned to work at two different centers that were following events in China. Peter Lee, John and Rita England, and Deng Zhaoming were my colleagues at the Tao Fong Shan Ecumenical Centre, along with a host of other associates working on China and emerging theologies in Asia. The United Methodists ran the China Liaison Office, and there I worked with Bud Carroll, Theresa Mei-fen Chu, and DeWitt Barnett. In between work at both places, I was supposed to be writing my dissertation, but this was a project that I never seemed to have time for. Too much was happening in China.

Nanjing

A delegation of Chinese Protestant leaders visited Hong Kong in the spring of 1981, and I was again invited to serve as interpreter and liaison. At this meeting, K. H. Ting told Janice and me that we would be invited to teach in the Department of Foreign Languages and Literatures at Nanjing University, a subject that had first been raised during the visit of the Chinese delegation to Princeton in 1979. In fact, I went to Nanjing that May to replace a Canadian teacher whose wife had fallen ill. I remember very well the train ride into Guangzhou and from there the flight to Nanjing, where I arrived on May 4, 1981. Janice and Elisabeth would not join me there until August.

Nanjing in the early 1980s was still emerging from the difficult years of the Cultural Revolution. There were not yet free markets in the cities, and our only contact with the outside world was radio broadcasts, the mail, and reports from visitors. Life was quite simple, and relationships with friends, students, and colleagues were very important. I had taken a leave of absence as a Presbyterian mission coworker so that there would be no misunderstanding about our role and presence in China. Between 1981 and 1983, Janice and I were employees of the Foreign Experts Bureau of the Chinese State Council. We had a continuing flow of foreign and Chinese visitors in our home in the "foreign experts" building.

Although I was no longer a missionary, everyone knew that we were Christians, and we attended Mo Chou Road Church every Sunday. I also visited the recently reopened Nanjing Theological Seminary regularly, and we got to know quite a few students and faculty members there. When I received permission to use the library, I began to read about the church and the Three-Self Movement in the 1940s and 1950s. Slowly my idea for a dissertation began to take better shape. I became interested in how Chinese Christians related to the new order after 1949, especially those who identified themselves with the United Front that was led by the Chinese

Communist Party. I was interested in the way in which they interpreted their faith in a new social context, and how this led them to become increasingly involved in the efforts to build up a new China. I also became aware of how Christians were adversely affected by the policies of the new order from the beginning, and especially during the years from the onset of the Anti-Rightist Movement in 1958 to the end of the Cultural Revolution almost twenty years later.

No one helped me to understand the danger of ultraleftism among Christians better than K. H. Ting, and I visited him regularly. He was interested in catching up on theological developments in the West over the last quarter century, and we had many hours of conversation about theology and the church. He would also give me his perspective on developments in China, on the church and religious policy, on new initiatives in culture and society, and on the ongoing struggle against "leftism." Like many students of my generation, I was fascinated by the Chinese Revolution, which inspired liberation movements in many other parts of the world as well as movements for social change on college campuses all over the world. K. H. advised me to be wary of what he termed "petit-bourgeois radicalism" as he spoke of the need for a more practical and incremental approach to change. Chinese intellectuals and Chinese Christians who had been attacked by Red Guards and ultraleftists during the Cultural Revolution welcomed Deng Xiaoping's new emphasis on practice. "The leftists begin not with facts, but with definitions," K. H. observed. "They want today what they cannot have until tomorrow."

Others at the university and the seminary made similar observations, and they taught me a great deal about what had really been happening in China since 1949. Their stories were sobering accounts of the costs of the social movements of the 1950s and 1960s. It was also clear, even in the early 1980s, that Christianity was now reemerging as a vigorous movement from below. Churches were being opened or reopened at the rate of two or more a day, especially in rural areas. Students and intellectuals were interested in learning more about Christian ideas. And although there were still many problems, "winter had passed and spring had returned" to China, to quote from a hymn written by Wang Weifan, a poet-theologian at Nanjing Theological Seminary.

It was still unclear how churches from overseas would respond to all of this. In 1981, the Canada China Program organized a conference in Montreal on "God's Call to a New Beginning: An International Dialogue with the Chinese Church." This was a historic meeting between Catholic and Protestant church leaders from China with more than 150 Christians from around the world. The fact that the Canadians had played such an important role in relating to Christians in China since the 1950s made the conference possible in the first place. I flew to Montreal from Nanjing to attend the conference and again assisted the Chinese with interpretation and liaison work. The most important thing about this gathering was that it introduced China to the complexities of the ecumenical world and that it made clear to churches overseas that future relationships with China had to mean a new beginning, not a return to the pre-1949 missionary era. The conference emphasized a contextual starting point for theology and church life, underscored by the presence of prominent third world theologians.[4]

We left Nanjing in the summer of 1983 and returned to Princeton, where I worked on my dissertation for the next twelve months. Charles West and Lynn White III, who taught Chinese politics at Princeton University, helped me shape the ideas that went into my dissertation, which represented a different point of departure from earlier studies of Christianity in China. I was particularly concerned with the way in which Christians were able to come together to help root the church in Chinese soil, a task foreign missionaries had not been able to do. Despite all of the difficulties they had been through, despite all of the problems with "leftism" in both the government and the Three-Self Movement itself, and despite all of the tensions in the church, Christianity in China is now more accessible to the average Chinese and the church more acceptable in Chinese society. This has been due largely to the church leaders who emerged in the Three-Self Movement after 1949 and again after 1979. My thesis has been widely debated among Christians and academics, but by and large I stand by what I wrote then.[5]

A short while before we left Nanjing, K. H. Ting invited me to his home and asked me what I had learned during my stay in China. "You may find it odd for me to say this," I replied, "but I can say that my faith has become more 'orthodox' in theology and practice, and I attribute this to how I have been formed by my experience in and with the Chinese Church." He replied with a smile, "That has been the experience of all of us over the last thirty years."

What I had learned in China involved a new understanding and a reaffirmation of what I first encountered in seminary. First articulated by Karl Barth and reworked in different ways by Lehmann and Shaull, as well as by many of the Asian Christians I had come to know, this perspective meant that one can be on the "right" theologically and on the "left" politically. In so doing, we can affirm without embarrassment that to which the Bible and the creeds point, and at the same time work creatively on the cutting-edge social and political issues of our times. In the process we make choices and we improvise. Because we have not reached "the end of history," what we affirm and the relationships in which we stand still matter.

Amity

It seemed that I had been preparing my whole life for my work with the Amity Foundation. Janice and I returned to Hong Kong in the fall of 1984, and a few weeks later, I traveled back to Nanjing. It was during this visit that K. H. Ting and Han Wenzao began speaking to me about their idea to create an organization with other reform-minded individuals outside the church. Its purpose would be to work for the betterment of society, to serve as a channel for international sharing and people-to-people relationships, and to make Christianity better known to the Chinese people. Over the next few months the groundwork was prepared, and in early 1985, I was asked to serve as Amity's overseas coordinator, seconded by the Presbyterian Church. What was initially a part-time position soon became an overwhelming task as I worked with a creative group of Christian leaders and a dedicated staff in Nanjing and Hong Kong.[6]

For most of the next twelve years, I spent much of my time shuttling between Hong Kong and Nanjing, developing and planning programs, and visiting teachers and projects in different parts of China. I developed a good working relationship with Han Wenzao, who was and is Amity's general secretary. He had an incredible way of transforming ideas into workable projects and programs, and worked hard to develop and inspire an energetic staff. We had outstanding people in Nanjing and Hong Kong, and from my experience in China, I learned that a good part of my work was listening to and being with them, and making it possible for them to make the best possible contribution they could to the common effort. I also learned a great deal about mission and social development, and, at least at the beginning, I was involved in all aspects of our program. As Amity developed, I was increasingly bogged down with responsibilities for administration and finance, which left me with less time for the writing, teaching, and speaking about China and the church that I so enjoyed.

Space does not permit a review of all aspects of my involvement with the Amity Foundation, but a brief excerpt from what I wrote on the tenth anniversary of its founding will suggest the ways in which my work in those years shaped my understanding of mission:

Ten years ago, the Amity Foundation was a venture in faith taken by Chinese Christian leaders and their supporters in the broader society.

Amity initially sought to assist projects which were "deserving of support, but inadequately funded." But the staff had no experience in working in the areas of rural development, welfare work and social service. Today, Amity staff members spend up to one third of their time on the road, overseeing projects in a variety of areas which are making important contributions to social development in China. Most of these are now in some of the poorest regions, particularly in the southwest. Ten years ago, we welcomed our first group of twenty-two teachers to China. . . . Today, we have eighty foreign teachers, most of whom serve in teacher training colleges in small cities. . . . Ten years ago, many people questioned whether the Amity Printing Press, a joint venture with the United Bible Societies, would really print any Bibles at all. No one asks that question now that total Bible production is over nine million.[7]

Amity represents a form of sharing in which Christians and non-Christians, from within China and overseas, can work together for the common good of the Chinese people. The unifying idea is love and the power of love to contribute to social development and strengthen international people-to-people relationships.

Christian faith as an embodiment of love has been a formative experience for Chinese Christians and for my own understanding of mission. K. H. Ting speaks of love as God's primary attribute, and this understanding is reflected in the work and witness of the Amity Foundation. It also has implications for initiatives from overseas. Paul's statement that "love does not insist on its way" (1 Cor. 13:5) should become a watchword for the international missionary involvement of any church. This, plus my continuing commitment to the Three-Self idea, which I first learned from Roland Allen, meant for me an approach to mission that emphasized friendship and cooperation.

My growing involvement with Amity was accompanied by an inward spiritual journey as well. The vitality of the Protestant experience in China was inspiring, but it reflected the spirituality of rural peasants who had only recently come to Christian faith. I needed to move in new directions, and I could find little help in the Presbyterian and Reformed piety of my own tradition. I increasingly turned to the writings of the mystics, and I became more interested in the Catholic, Orthodox, and Anglican approach to worship and prayer. James McCord had once told me "that to be Reformed is to be catholic and to be Catholic is to be reformed," and I began to experience this in my own life and work.

For the first time in my life, I also felt called to the ordained ministry. The Chinese church was a church of the laity, but there was a desperate shortage of pastors. In this situation, I saw the importance of an ordained minister as a center of church unity, holding together the sacramental ministry of the church. While maintaining a firm commitment to the ministry of the laity, I now saw that ordination would make possible my own increasing involvement in the church at the local level. I spoke with K. H. Ting about my sense of call, and he asked if I would consider being ordained in China. This was something I wanted, because I had been in many ways formed by the Chinese church, but never thought was possible. A lengthy process of consultation followed, concluding with a retreat with the five Chinese who would be ordained at the same time. On April 28, 1991, I became the first non-Chinese to be ordained in China's postdenominational church. For me, this sealed my ecumenical approach to mission and ministry. Bishop Peter Kwong authorized my service in Christ Church, Kowloon Tong (part of the Anglican diocese), and I also became a member of the Presbytery of Hudson River, where my journey had begun.

San Anselmo

Although there is a part of me that never wanted to leave China (and a part that never will), I had become impatient with the administrative side of my work. In the late 1990s, several Presbyterian seminaries began looking for people to teach mission and world Christianity and I was contacted by their search committees. Because of my long involvement in Asia, I was convinced that I could only go to a seminary that had a common interest and vision. This made San Francisco Theological Seminary the only real possibility, and so I accepted the call to come to San Anselmo as the Flora Lamson Hewlett Professor of Evangelism and Mission in January 1998. The diversity of the Bay area, the affiliation with the Graduate Theological Union, and the possibility for me to maintain my involvement in Asia helped to confirm my choice.

Mainline churches and seminaries in the United States have developed a renewed interest in world mission over the last few years. This in part reflects a genuine interest in embracing what used to be called "the globalization of theological education" and the need to relate to our multicultural world in new ways. But it also reflects the crisis the denominations are experiencing with regard to their own social location in American society. The rediscovery of world mission is one aspect of the neoconservative turn in the culture of our churches, and, as a result, the widely touted "paradigm shift" has in some ways meant a shift backwards. In contrast, I believe that we are in need of a new starting point, one that will encourage churches in North America to see themselves in mission as part of the worldwide body of Christ, but not necessarily as the most important actors. We should not regard the tremendous resources we have at our disposal as something to be exploited, but rather, in humble obedience, seek to discover what it means to be the people of God among all God's peoples.

Paul Lehmann used to say that the future creates the present out of the past. The vision that has emerged from my twenty-three years in Asia now shapes my approach to teaching mission, and this has three direct implications for what I am doing.

First, mission must be at the center of the theological enterprise.[8] We have been reminded in recent years that mission is the mother of theology. Martin Kähler's words have a particular emphasis: "The oldest mission became the mother of theology because it attacked the existing culture."[9] He is stressing the critical function of mission and theology. In this sense, the New Testament is a missionary document because it reflects the critical response of the church to a crisis situation. It is the record of a theology written on the move. Similarly, contextual theologies in Asia are "missionary theologies" in a sense that most European and North American theologies are not. They cross frontiers in response to the new social and cultural situations their churches are facing.

We are encountering our own crisis situation in North America for which we need our own contextualized theologies. The church needs to move in new directions, and this requires a renewed commitment to mission. Seminary students need to develop an understanding of the church as a community sent out in God's mission to the world. Theological education must combine critical reflection, spiritual formation, and the acquisition of the arts and skills of ministry; all of these are needed in any course on mission. The study of mission necessarily combines theory and practice, producing a kind of practical reasoning that calls us into a future which does not yet exist. This is why I like Ivan Illich's description of missiology as the study of the church in its becoming, the Word made flesh in borderline situations, the church as a surprise.

Second, as we struggle with paradigm shifts and the surprises we face in the mission of the church, it has become increasingly clear that there can be no single all embracing new paradigm of mission. In the foregoing pages, I have spoken of the people and places and issues that have formed me in mission in very particular ways. These weave together the fabric of mission, and form the social extension of the incarnation in a given time. For me, the word that comes closest to describing the way in which these are brought together is *hospitality*. The woven fabric is placed upon a table around which people are gathered for a common meal to which all are invited. Hospitality is a universal cultural form that involves a living encounter of peoples.

Christian hospitality is not exclusivist or imposed on others. It suggests instead that in mission we are related to everyone, everyone is welcome, everyone has a role to play. Hospitality involves face-to-face encounters, not abstractions. This implies a kind of mutual indwelling, a theology of the image of God in people, of God's love, of the Spirit of Christ that is both universal and particular, and therefore incarnational. It suggests a servant Christology, a servanthood that produces a theology among friends. As Christians involved in mission, we make endless improvisations, and because we cannot predict things in advance, we are often surprised. There are a variety of people writing about hospitality these days from different perspectives, and it has emerged for me as a theme in mission out of my own life experience in a missionary situation. It is a theme that is more adequately expressed in the sharing of narratives rather than in the construction of propositional statements.

Third, mission as hospitality means that we need to create a more hospitable world. In this light, the two issues that I see as central to my work as a theological educator are globalization and plurality. Globalization, the integration of the world into a single market economy facilitated by advances in telecommunications and the end of the Cold War, has brought the world closer together, and offers creative possibilities for mission and social development. At the same time, globalization has become an ideology dominated by powerful interests that marginalize and exclude the majority of the world's population and presents itself as a realized secular eschatology. How the phenomenon of globalization affects our churches and shapes our understanding of mission are issues that will be with us for many years to come. Religious and cultural plurality are in one sense the other side of globalization, reflecting the particularity and diversity of local communities and different cultures. In what sense is plurality part of God's intention for the created order? To what extent does it reflect both the relatedness and relativity of all cultures? How can we embrace a "reconciled diversity" in our understanding of mission? These are the questions I pose to my students as among the most urgent missiological challenges facing churches today.

In the church where Janice and I worship, we are fond of quoting Gregory of Nyssa, who said that friendship with God is the goal of Christian life. We can extend this to say that mission is a journey between friends, through which we are called to become coworkers in God's mission to the world. Mission, which begins with an act of reception, is a continuing movement that involves the redrawing of boundaries and the discovery of the meaning of the gospel in new situations. Mission means that we shall not cease from exploration. I think this is what Paul was suggesting when he wrote, "But I am still running, trying to capture that by which I have been captured" (Phil. 3:12, [author's translation]). In this way, the journey continues.

NOTES

1. From "Little Gidding," in T. S. Eliot, *The Four Quartets* (London: Faber & Faber, 1986), 48.

2. Eugene Rosenstock-Huessy, *I Am an Impure Thinker* (Norwich, Ver.: Argo Books, 1970), 2.

3. See Roland Allen, *Missionary Methods, St. Paul's or Ours?* (Grand Rapids: Eerdmans, 1960). First published in 1912, this book is still in print today.

4. Theresa Chu and Christopher Lind, eds., *A New Beginning* (Toronto: Canada China Programme, 1983).

5. My dissertation was later published as *Seeking the Common Ground: Protestant Christianity, the Three-Self Movement and China's United Front* (Maryknoll, N.Y.: Orbis, 1988).

6. See my "Development Service and China's Modernization: The Amity Foundation in Theological Perspective," *Ecumenical Review* 41, no. 1 (January 1989): 78–87.

7. By the end of 1999, the Amity Printing Press had produced almost 23 million Bibles.

8. The phrase is from "The People of God among All God's Peoples: Frontiers in Christian Mission," a report from the mission roundtable called by the Christian Conference of Asia and the Council for World Mission, November 10–17, 1999.

9. As quoted in David Bosch, *Transforming Mission: Paradigm Shifts in the Theology of Mission* (Maryknoll, N.Y.: Orbis, 1991), 16.

PART IV

Mission as Church-with-Others

Asian Spirituality and Christian Mission

In January 1987, I visited Thailand, Burma (Myanmar), and Singapore while in the middle of my doctoral studies at Princeton Theological Seminary. I do not recommend such a foolish move. With comprehensive exams behind me, all I had to do was write a dissertation and I would be finished. What makes my move even more foolish is that I knew the statistics regarding students who start Ph.D. programs compared with those who finish. Roughly half never finish, and for those who leave their school of study the statistics are even worse. With this knowledge firmly ignored, I headed off to do a series of lectures at the Bangkok Institute of Theology, and then to study the missionary and church contexts of Burma and Singapore. To be honest, I had a couple of good friends at Princeton, one from Rangoon and the other from Singapore, who insisted that as long as I was going to Thailand, for just a few more dollars . . . I was given gifts to take to one Burmese student's wife and a letter to take to a Singapore student's friend. The letter was no problem. The gifts, however, included vitamins ("My wife is very sick and she cannot get enough food because of the economy."), shoes, a few hundred-dollar bills, and three bras.

These items created a little uneasiness as I began packing my bag. Travel in Burma in the 1980s was just beginning to open up, and so customs agents were very particular about what a person could bring into the country. They were in the habit of opening every suitcase and bag. Were vitamins drugs? What about the shoes? Would they ask if they were mine? Would they fit if I had to prove that they were mine? How did the Burmese government feel about cross-dressing? Should I try to hide the bras, or just pack them in with my own clothes and

/ 111

shaving cream? To add to my anxiety, I decided while I was in Bangkok that it would be a noble thing to bring in some Burmese Bibles and a couple of Greek New Testaments.

As the plane from Bangkok was preparing to land in Rangoon, I placed the greenbacks in the bottom of my shoe. Within seconds they were wet with perspiration. What happens if they ask me to take off my shoes? I began to pray and to rehearse mentally. "No, sir. That is my wife's bra. You see, we are traveling together, but she stayed back in Bangkok while I am spending a few days in your lovely city." "No sir, I don't know who put those Bibles there. It must be some type of capitalist plot. You know how evil those capitalist pigs are." As the plane landed, my thoughts of denial and excuses faded away and I had a sudden calm that, for all of my inexperience and naivete, God was with me as I traveled simply to encourage some Christians in Burma. Going through customs, nothing was said about my strange wardrobe, or about my bottles of vitamins, or about my five Burmese Bibles. Neither did anyone ask me to take off my shoes.

I arrived on a Saturday and on Sunday I was ushered off to a worship service of over five hundred ethnic Chin Baptists who had migrated from the western mountains to the capital. Two things struck me about the worship service: it was so similar to Christian worship everywhere in the world and it was so new and strange for me. The similarities were obvious: wonderful singing with guitars, prayers, scripture reading, exhortation, and many prayers of thanksgiving. I remember asking my translator at one point what the pastor had just prayed for. "He is thanking God for the freedom we have to worship and share the good news in Burma," came the reply. Such joy and thanksgiving in a Buddhist/socialist/military state! But this two-and-a-half hour worship service was also very different. The large assembly hall was not a church building and was in a terrible state of disrepair. There were various nonhuman mammals walking throughout the building and there were no hymnals or Bibles (except for a few that were used for liturgical reading). What impressed me the most was the spirit of the people I met. Here I was, a rich Westerner, and everyone I met asked me to take back greetings, thanked me for coming, and asked me to have Americans pray for them. (I promised I would, so please do.)

Since the mid-1960s, it has been illegal for foreign missionaries to reside in Burma, or for foreigners to preach or teach without government permission. (I knew this because I had read the Lonely Planet guide.) Toward the end of the worship service I was called on to bring greetings from the United States. My interpreter reassured me that as long as I paused every few minutes and said, "and I bring greetings from the Christians in New York (or Toledo)," everything would be okay and I could speak for fifteen or twenty minutes. Then he added that they would like to have a sermon. I slowly walked up the aisle with my interpreter, feeling very tall and very blonde. When I got to the pulpit I turned to the congregation and just about fainted. Over five hundred Chin, many in their ethnic dress, stared silently, waiting for a word from the Lord. Even the dogs seemed to stop their foraging. What should I say? What do I have to offer? Suddenly it became clear. I have nothing to offer but Jesus Christ crucified and raised from the dead. So I gave my testimony ("and I bring greetings from my wife in Bangkok") and told about Jesus' obedience unto death ("and I bring greetings from my parents in Wisconsin") and how his resurrection and ascension brings us life ("and I bring you greetings from Princeton Theological Seminary"). Some of the people had tears in their eyes as I finished. I was overwhelmed, but before I stepped down I promised that I would tell the church in America to pray for them.

I would like to jump ahead now to 1996. After moving back to the United States in 1995, I returned to teach a one-month course in Singapore in July 1996. I took a four-day holiday to visit some of my former students who were planting an Anglican church in Phnom Penh, Cambodia. The Singaporean pastor hired transportation for me for one day to take me to various sites in the city. I had no idea where I was going, and my chauffeur's English was only slightly better than my Khmer (nonexistent). Even if his English had been clear, I could have heard very little he was telling me since he was in front of me on the motorcycle.

Of the many places we visited, one stands out. A small Roman Catholic church located on the east side of the Mekong River made quite an impression on me. This is a floodplain area and the people are among the most poor in one of the world's poorest countries. The "church" was a house with a preschool/social service center/sanctuary on the dirt floor. Children would come in to get help with reading or math. Lay workers would pray with them, sing songs, and give them snacks. It was hot, steamy, dirty, and full of mosquitoes—but it was glorious. The people were filled with joy and purpose as they served their local community. I prayed with the priest, jumped on the back of the motorcycle, and returned to Christ our Peace Anglican Church.

In the course of my eight years' teaching at Trinity Theological College in Singapore, I also had the opportunity to visit seminaries, churches, and church agencies in Japan, China, Korea, the Philippines, Indonesia, India, Malaysia, and Pakistan. Most of these trips were related to research on Asian church history, or were preaching and teaching opportunities. In all of these travels, what I have learned has had more to do with spirituality than with history or missiology. To be more accurate, these experiences have confirmed a theological understanding I had taught in Asia, but had not completely understood: Worship and mission are inseparable. Worship overflows into mission. The joy of God's Yes on our behalf cannot be contained, but must be shared with others. To put it in the negative, a spirituality that does not overflow into mission is self-centered or culturally bound. Paul's benediction at the end of his letter to the Romans expresses this. Although this is an expression of worship, it cannot hold back the missionary impulse. Paul is overwhelmed as he reflects on the missionary God: "Now to him who is able to establish you by my gospel and the proclamation of Jesus Christ, according to the revelation of the mystery hidden for long ages past, but now revealed and made known through the prophetic writings by the command of the eternal God, so that all nations might believe and obey him—to the only wise God be glory forever through Jesus Christ! Amen" (Rom. 16:25–27).

What follows is a description of how, through my mission involvement in Asia, I have come to rethink Christian mission in four broad areas. I present these four areas here as four couplets of characteristics: humility and hospitality, suffering and simplicity, scripture and clarity, and zeal and consistency. The memory of many of the people who have taught me these themes continues to guide me today. In fact, the faces and conversations come back to me as if to remind me to "keep the course" even in the West. In conclusion, I will provide some ways that my teaching and pastoral work in a seminary setting have been influenced by these associations.

Humility and Hospitality

I like to think that I come from a Christian people in America who are gracious and hospitable, but as most people who travel around the world will confirm, the hospitality of Arabs, Indians, Burmese, and other non-Western people is overwhelming. It seems that in every place I stopped in East or South Asia I was offered a cup of tea or coffee even before I was sure about my surroundings. Guests are to be cared for. Travelers must be provided for. No matter how simple the meal or meager the snack, the hospitality of my various hosts has changed me. Not only the fact of hospitality, but the humble attitude of servanthood is a part of this same trait. Both the hospitality and the humility communicate, "You are more important than I." I distinctly remember occasions in Thailand, Burma, and Pakistan talking to a few pastors around cups of tea and biscuits and then suddenly feeling so small as I would hear of the ministries performed, or the suffering endured by my hosts. I was once introduced to a pastor whom I later found out had planted churches in four different regions of the country and was now starting a Bible college to train tribal church leaders and evangelists. Often I would find out such information only after a few hours of conversation. The pioneering ministries of many of my friends in Asia are quite remarkable. If their ministries had taken place in the United States, they would be awarded honorary degrees and be featured speakers at church growth and "seekers" conferences. But these stories usually had to be coaxed out of my humble friends.

Jenny was a pastor from Myanmar (Burma) who, after waiting for nearly fifteen years, was finally sent to do an advanced degree in Singapore.* She had stayed in Myanmar even as many men had gone ahead of her to the United States or England to study. When she was finally permitted to go, she did not get to go to the West. She merely flew three hours to the island state of Singapore. Jenny was very quiet, she had numerous health problems, and she struggled with the studies at the seminary, but she persisted in spite of these factors. One day, after about three months of study, Jenny sat in our living room and began to tell some of us about her experience as a pastor in Myanmar. This quiet, nervous, and (so we thought) fragile pastor had opposed government officials and soldiers to protect church property. She literally stood guard to make sure that the army did not remove the church property fence. She won. In addition, she had been a missionary to an unreached people in the Shan state where she planted a church. During this time, she would only visit her husband and children infrequently since travel was so time-consuming and so expensive.

With a quiet but strong humility, Jenny had endured and persisted in ways most of us will never have to. This moment of being surprised by the depth of experience and suffering of those around me was repeated over and over again. I am reminded of Paul's admonition to the Corinthians: "But we have this treasure in jars of clay to show that this all-surpassing power is from God and not from us. We are hard pressed on every side, but not crushed; perplexed, but not in despair, persecuted, but not abandoned, struck down, but not destroyed. We always carry around in our body the death of Jesus, so that the life of Jesus may also be revealed in our body" (2 Cor. 4:7–10).

Suffering and Simplicity

A second area of church life in Asia that changed my thinking about mission is also represented by a pair of traits. In most all of Asia, the

---

*Some names have been changed here and on the following pages.

suffering and simplicity of Christian witness is remarkable for those of us from the West. Even in the affluent, modern, high-tech city-state of Singapore, the church suffers when its mission to the poor and outcasts is perceived as a threat to those in power. We have to remember that in Asia only the Philippines has a Christian majority. In most every country, Christians live under some type of restrictions (e.g., it is against the law to give a Bible to a Malay), or intermittent persecution (China, Myanmar) or consistent persecution (North Korea, Laos). When people are baptized and identify with Jesus Christ, it may very well be perceived as a political statement or as a rejection of family.

In my first year of teaching in Singapore, I met a theology student who was raised as a Muslim. I asked him about his conversion and learned that his story was a series of chapters of rejection and persecution. Persecution first came from his family, then from the Singapore police (who perceived him as a threat to social order), and then from the local Muslim community. In the end, he had to move away from his family and to request the police, who earlier had persecuted him, to protect him. It would be an insult to ask this young man if it were all worth it. Following Jesus has been costly, but it has been joyous. He now has a ministry, a quiet and careful ministry, to other Muslim converts in the region. "So then, death is at work in us, but life is at work in you" (2 Cor. 4:12, NRSV).

I believe this particular pastor is still alive, but for many in Asia, the persecution ends in martyrdom. The suffering of Christians in the past fifty years in Asia deserves a whole chapter in the history of Christianity. In the early 1970s, the church was beginning to grow in Cambodia. Churches were being built and pastors were being trained to accommodate the thousands of new believers. Suddenly Pol Pot came to power and Christians were scattered, murdered, and imprisoned. In Vietnam, many Christians in the North fled to the South after the Communist takeover. When the country was reunited under the North Vietnamese government, many Christians fled, but many church leaders were imprisoned or killed. I could continue by mentioning, for example, the rise of Kim Il Sung in North Korea, the persecution of Christians in Laos, Nepal, Pakistan, and Indonesia, and then we would have to devote a huge space for the sufferings of Christians in China. Since the earliest stories and legends of Christians in Asia, martyrdom has been a common theme.

Not only in dramatic ways, where the family rejects a Christian son or daughter, or the father tries to kill a Christian child, or the government "detains" a young convert, but even more so in smaller, more subtle, and persistent ways, Christians in Asia are restricted. I had never worried about what an Internal Security Department official would think of my sermon until I preached in Singapore. The thought had never occurred to me before that my phones might be tapped, or that conversations about evangelism or social concerns should be held outside since the restaurant or taxi might be bugged. Government restrictions and "oversight" are very subtle but persistent in most countries in Asia. If it is not the government, then local religious or ethnic communities may suppress Christians out of fear of conversions. The daily consciousness of the political nature of religious faith changed the way I thought about my own Christian life. Should I speak up concerning injustices I saw around me? Should I mention the evangelistic responsibilities that the church bears on behalf of the Muslim and the Hindu? Was it better to be silent, to keep these things to myself? The backdrop and possibility of suffering gives a shading or spiritual dynamic to Asian Christians that is nearly ineffable, but nonetheless real.

Closely related to the suffering of the church in Asia is the simplicity of life and worship in most countries. In addition to the tenuous nature of Christian existence in Asia, the widespread poverty reinforces the simplicity of Christian living. There are places in Asia where the church is prospering with limited restrictions (Taiwan, Singapore, South Korea), but for the most part the church cannot accumulate much in the way of worldly goods. The church is not "comfortable" in this world. Travel to neighboring villages is a complex affair, but since personal possessions are light and inconsequential, travel is much less complicated than it might otherwise be. In 1987, I was visiting a local village church in northern Thailand one Sunday, a village with a new Christian community in an area where the Buddhist presence bordered on the militant. The Christian community was a very close-knit group. The Sunday I worshiped with them, however, an older farmer was missing from worship. It was decided that "we" should go on a pastoral call to inquire about the farmer's health. Eight of us, I being the only visitor, jumped on four motorcycles and headed off on what appeared to be a dry creek bed. I was told later that it was the road. After forty-five minutes we arrived on the edge of nowhere, and the farmer came out of his hut. He invited us in for tea and explained that he was not feeling well. The local pastor delivered a slightly reduced version of the sermon, we prayed for the man, and jumped back on the motorcycles. Things, or even the lack of things, did not interfere with the first concern: people. We took nothing with us on our afternoon call except for two or three Bibles. The farmer's life was very simple; his possessions seemed to consist of a small hut on stilts, a motorcycle, pots and pans, and his Bible.

Scripture and Clarity

While walking to church in Singapore one Sunday I had one of those cross-cultural jolts that moves one to ponder. On a nice new Mercedes-Benz were two bumper stickers: *Read the Koran* and *Have you read the Koran today?* A command and a question; exhortation and inquisition. This was the type of tacky proselytizing of which I thought only Christians were capable. It was a gentle reminder, though, that we also are people of the Book. Closely related to the issues of suffering and simplicity is the centrality of the Bible in mission in Asia. Most of my students in Singapore and 93 percent of my congregants were converts from other religious beliefs. The Bible seemed to be much more important and was held in much higher regard than in the West. Please don't misunderstand me, this is not a conservative or fundamentalist tendency. This is a deep regard and respect for the Bible as God's Word. This is not "bibleolotry" or literalism, for those issues have bypassed most of the Christian communities in Asia. It is much deeper or even more mystical than that. To put it in an Asian perspective, the Bible is the Holy Book and is respected as such. There is a clarity about Christian identity related to the plain reading of the scriptural text.

A few examples may help. I still have vivid memories of coming to class in Singapore, ready to give a lecture on Asian church history, and noticing that a good number of students who had arrived early were using the few moments before class to catch up on reading. For the most part they were all reading the Bible. There was a clarity about the Bible as the central authority in ministry and in personal decisions. Often I would start class by reading a Bible verse that would raise some of the issues to be discussed in the day's lecture. After reading the passage I would ask where the passage could be found in the Bible. Not all of the passages were as familiar as John 3:16, and yet there would always be a number of students who could identify the book and the chapter, even if they did not know the exact verses. The Bible was a part of their daily lives through reading, meditation, and decision making.

There are other small indicators that the Bible is a normative element in the lives, not just the Christian faith, of most Asian Christians. It is impressive, if not a little surprising, to attend worship in Korea and to see that everyone carries a Bible and hymnbook to worship. Personal devotions as well as public worship are both guided by these two books. In most Asian churches, people bring their Bibles to church (except for in countries where Bibles are not easily procured). When the morning's text is read, people automatically turn to the passage. The contrast was quite dramatic when I returned to the States. I still find it odd that in Christian churches where there is freedom to worship and where Bibles are plentiful, the liturgist will announce, "You can find this morning's passage on page 812 in your pew Bible." There is little clarity about the centrality of the Bible in most Western churches, and little familiarity. The Bible is treated as a foreign book, and so there is little confidence that the Bible is important for me each day in all that I do. For Christians in Asia, the Bible is valued. It is treasured and it is read with a sense of expectancy, even urgency.

Zeal and Consistency

I believe that a person's religion can be identified by looking at that person's checkbook or by finding out what preoccupies him or her. What people think about as they ride on the bus, what they look forward to, what they talk about when they get together with other friends—these are windows into the religious soul. I found among seminary students and the members of my church in Singapore a holy preoccupation with the things of the kingdom. Their concern was, more specifically, a missionary passion. There were many ways that this preoccupation was seen. Let me offer a few illustrations.

I spoke to many potential students about going to seminary, both young people from Singapore and those from the surrounding regions of South and Southeast Asia. A large percentage of these seminary candidates were thinking of going to seminary or Bible college to prepare for missionary service. The matter was of such a concern for me that I—a missionary and a trained missiologist—found myself taking a number of people out to fine eight- and ten-course Chinese meals to try to convince them *not* to go into missionary work. There was more interest in missionary work than in local pastoral work. I was of two minds in this "mission" of mine, knowing that missionary work is a noble service ordained by God, but also knowing that these churches growing so rapidly in Asia needed pastors. Was I being too shortsighted? Was I being a missionary of little faith?

But the singlemindedness was more than just a passion to go to a foreign country and start churches, it was also a passion for mission in the neighborhood, the local communities, and to those a step-and-a-half away. In my pastoral work in Singapore, a constant concern in our session meetings was witnessing to parents. Most of the church members were converts, which meant that most of the parents and a good number of the siblings were either Buddhist or some type of Chinese religionist. Chinese in Singapore have come from many different regions of China and so many different dialects are still spoken by the older folks (e.g., Teo Chew, Hokkein, Cantonese). The church would plan small trips for the Teo Chew parents, with a local Presbyterian pastor who spoke that dialect. The next month there would be a picnic for Cantonese parents with a Cantonese-speaking pastor to give a brief message.

Holidays were also a clear indication of the heavenly preoccupation of my parishioners. Christian youth plan "camps" during the holidays. These events are seldom held in camps as we think of them, for Singapore is a fairly urban environment. Still, camp-like activities (games, hiking, crafts, singing) are held, but the central theme in these youth camps is usually evangelistic. Students work hard to get non-Christian friends to attend. The results are quite impressive, for the longer a young person is in school in Singapore, the greater the chance that he or she will become a Christian. It seems that this preoccupation with mission to friends has an impact over the years. I remember on numerous occasions, secondary and tertiary students would ask me to pray for their friends whom they were bringing to camp during the school holidays. These friends would be Buddhist, Hindu, Muslim, and "free thinkers." What impressed me was the preoccupation that these young people had about bringing their friends to the cross. Teenagers, parents, seminary students—all had a zeal to bring people into the kingdom. Sometimes, though, this zeal would become a little awkward.

On a trip to interview some potential graduate students in Myanmar, a colleague of mine, Dr. David Wu, and I were staying at the old Strand Hotel. One of our students from Myanmar was also back in Yangon (Rangoon) for the school holiday, and when he found out we were in the area he invited us to see his "missionary training center," which happened to be just a few blocks from the hotel. This was not one of our best students, and we were both rather surprised to find out that he was the director of such a center. One morning, after tea, soft-boiled eggs, and toast, we walked down the street to the center. We passed a number of soldiers, for this was soon after the democracy uprising in 1989. We also passed the Buddhist Missionary Society, whose purpose, I later found out, is to try to convert the tribal peoples to Buddhism before they become Christian. Finally, we came to the mission center and, sure enough, there in an open storefront were forty-some people sitting in chairs listening to our student as he led a Bible study. When he saw us he ran to greet us, told the class there would be a five-minute break, and gave us a quick tour of his facility. He then asked us each to give a Bible lesson. I will never forget the conglomerate of fear, excitement, and joy that flooded my mind as I stood up, facing the open storefront, looking at tribal people from all over Myanmar and then noticing a number of soldiers stopping to look in as I began to talk about the incarnation (it was Advent). Sentence by sentence our student would translate as his students took notes and looked up passages in their Bibles, while the soldiers rested their rifles on their shoulders. I thought about the joy of our salvation, but at the same time I thought about how nice it would be to see my family again. How difficult it is to be zealous for one thing. Again and again this consistent zeal for the mission of God was evident in the Christian communities in Asia.

Back in the States

Daily interactions today with seminary students and friends in churches remind me over and over how different Christian awareness and self-understanding are in the United States from that in most Asian countries. As I mentioned earlier in this piece, it seems that the intersecting themes of worship and mission point out that our real concern is spirituality. What does it mean to be in Christ, to be a redeemed person? I have pointed out four elements of this Asian spirituality (humility and hospitality, suffering and simplicity, scripture and clarity, zeal and consistency). I believe that these themes challenge us in the West today. I am overwhelmed by the contrasts, but I am not without hope. The missional spirituality I observed in Asia has been a reminder of my own need to identify with Christ in more than just superficial ways. I have made some changes in the way I live and the way I teach in light of my Asian tutors.

First, I have taken prayer more seriously, without needing to understand it. I take it as a matter of simple obedience and humble submission to "pray without ceasing." I have made it a point, whenever possible, not to let students leave my office without praying for them. Nothing else I teach them or do with or for them may matter as much as a simple prayer. In addition, it has become necessary for me to see that teaching mission is as much an issue of the heart as it is a matter for the head. Thus, I "require" my students to develop, for at least one term, the habit of praying for the world. We learn about the needs and suffering in the world, and even though we cannot go and solve all of the problems (a very American "can do" attitude), we can do what is more important—lift up the pain and violence, the injustice and ignorance of our world to the Creator and Savior. I am learning to make prayer central in my teaching about Christian mission.

Second, I have been concerned by the lack of passion for mission and evangelism in the United States. It can be very depressing when I think that almost none of my students have an interest in serving as missionaries. The contrast with Asia, once again, is striking. In light of this situation, I have made it a priority to help future pastors in America get the opportunity to work with, talk with, and watch Christian leaders in the non-Western world. Sending our students overseas is a priority, but also bringing Christian leaders to the United States is helpful in imparting hope and vision to our future leaders. In my second year of teaching in the United States, we had a student from Indonesia who was studying at Pittsburgh Theological Seminary. As a way to introduce him to my mission class, I interviewed him to help students know what types of questions we should ask to learn from and support our international guests. I will never forget the expressions on the faces of our students when I asked this quiet little man how many people attended the church he was pastoring in Jakarta. "Oh, about three thousand." Without realizing it, most of us had assumed that since he was a little guy from Asia, he probably had a little storefront church. Most of our students will pastor churches that have less than one hundred on a given Sunday.

Finally, I have come to see that in our seminaries, we as faculty have become very selective in our globalization of theological education. We want to learn about social issues and we want to help educate non-Western students and pastors, but we are little interested in some of the deeper spiritual issues that drive the church in Asia. We are interested in injustices, military coups, and other religions, but the very thing we need is the very thing we shun—the spiritual life and the missionary passion of Asian Christians. Korean prayer meetings at five o'clock in the morning are more of an oddity or curiosity to us rather than a challenge to our very life and health as Christians. We continue to exhibit a quiet, self-satisfied paternalism when we hear about Asian missionary zeal. Typical of Western indifference to Asian spirituality and mission was the reception given to a Chinese Christian scholar who visited our seminary after I returned to the States. Christianity is growing very rapidly in China; this fact is known by all, even the Chinese government. Yet when our Chinese guest came to speak about the church in China, we had no interest in finding out about the development of China Christian Council churches or "underground" churches. We had no interest in the various missionary impulses in China, nor in the spiritual formation in local churches. Most of our questions were about the church-state issues. Did our guest see greater openness to the world both economically and politically, or would there be a reversal of this openness? I think most of us do not even know how to talk about spirituality and mission to people from China, Myanmar, Indonesia, or Vietnam. The West may still harbor imperial notions about the rest of the world and therefore be unable to hear the religious critique from churches that are growing and vital. The world has changed, and we in the West have not really accepted the fact that we have become a mission field.

In late January 2000, our local newspapers picked up an interesting story that illustrates some of the tensions and difficulties as we try to understand the spiritual and missionary concerns of Asia today. The archbishop of Singapore, the Most Rev. Dr. Moses Tay, was involved in a consecration of two "missionary bishops" who were sent back to the United States to "actively seek to plant Anglican missions in areas where there are receptive communities." The language sounds very similar to the language of the American Board of Commissioners for Foreign Missions as they sent out Adonirum and Ann Judson to India or Malaya or wherever they could establish a mission; it was a vague pioneering missionary commission to people who needed to learn to follow Jesus. Now missionaries are being sent to "post-Christian" rather than "pre-Christian" areas, and the bishops in the West are "appalled by this irregular action." I am not arguing here for the validity of Anglicans sending missionaries to the West or from the West. What is of interest for us is the perceived need of Asian (and African) Christians for the West to receive missionaries, and the expressed offense of the Western bishops. This "irregular action" can only be understood if we take the time to know and accept the spirituality and missionary passion of Asian Christians. Can it be that we have more to learn than to criticize? Maybe this action was more of a signpost than an "irregular action." May we have the grace to read the signs and the humility to learn and follow.

Learning to Listen

BONNIE SUE LEWIS

*T*his is a story without an ending. It began when I was in fifth grade and told my parents that I wanted to be a missionary—either that or a pioneer. Both had the allure of adventure and the excitement of travel. I don't think my parents were surprised. As a family we had done our share of camping, and as active Presbyterians we had hosted our share of visiting missionaries. I learned early that the call to mission was a worthy calling. What I needed to learn was that it is God's mission and God is the one who calls and who equips. In order to be a missionary, I had to first learn to listen to the triune God whose heart is for the people of his creation. Then I could begin to listen to God's creatures, to hear their heart cries, to bear witness to them of a Savior's love, to learn from them new ways of seeing and serving God. I am still learning. This is a story that isn't finished yet.

Listening to God

In my fourth year as assistant professor of mission and Native American Christianity at the University of Dubuque Theological Seminary, Dubuque, Iowa, I am only beginning to articulate the theology of mission that drives my teaching. I find at its heart the promise of Psalm 46:10: "Be still and know that I am God. I will be exalted among the nations, I will be exalted in the earth" (NIV). God is sovereign and it is his work of grace at work in the world. At the end of history all nations will be represented at God's throne. There they shall find healing and shall see God's face and worship him. This is God's doing. This is God's mission of love, God's calling of nations, the *missio Dei.*

The concept of the *missio Dei* was first expressed by Karl Barth at the Willingen Conference of the International Missionary Council in 1952. Grounded in Trinitarian theology and God's very nature, it pointed to an understanding of "God the Father sending the Son, and God the Father and the Son sending the Spirit [and] was expanded to include yet another 'movement': Father, Son and Holy Spirit sending the church into the world."[1] This understanding has led many in the church to conclude that mission is an attribute of God, that it is God's loving agency at work calling all people to himself. God is, in fact, a missionary God, and the church is called to participate in this calling by being the arms and feet of God to bring the good news of the gospel to a hurting world.

Since it is God's mission, it is imperative that the church recognize its role as "a community chosen to be the bearer of the secret of the kingdom."[2] We must, in both word and deed, bring others to Christ, not just to church, that they may find reconciliation with God and love, joy, peace, and hope in this world and the next. We are missionaries with God, through God, and by God's power. Therefore, we must have "the mind of Christ" and be able to hear what God is saying to the church.

I begin my classes with scripture reading and prayer. At the beginning of the term we usually start with reading the Great Commission in Matthew 28:18–20: "And Jesus came and said to them, 'All authority in heaven and on earth has been given to me. Go therefore and make disciples of all nations, baptizing them in the name of the Father and of the Son and of the Holy Spirit, teaching them to observe all that I have commanded you; and lo, I am with you always, to the close of the age'" (RSV). But we don't end there. We go on to what I have called "Isaiah's Great Admonition to the Great Commission," found in Isaiah 52:12: "For you shall not go out in haste, and you shall not go in flight; for the LORD will go before you, and the God of Israel will be your rear guard" (RSV). We are not to go running off to do God's mission in haste. Because it is God who goes before and behind, we must first "be still and know" the God who sends us. Knowing God, as J. I. Packer reminds us in his great book of that title, is what we were made for.[3] For Paul, knowing God was his most treasured possession. He concluded, "I regard everything as loss because of the surprising value of knowing Christ Jesus my Lord" (Phil. 3:8, NRSV). God is the friend of sinners, the one who made us, the one who loves us as no other. We begin by getting to know the God who sends us.

Knowing God releases and empowers us to do that to which he calls us. As Daniel discovered, it is "the people who know their God [who] shall stand firm and take action" (Dan. 11:32, RSV). Daniel and his friends could meet with derision and disaster and remain confident because they knew the God in whom they trusted. Uncertainty and pain could not undo them because their God was "strong to save." They could step out in faith, knowing that their God would see them through their ordeal. Because God was trustworthy and faithful they could boldly respond in obedience to his call, regardless of the outcome. Daniel and his friends began by listening to him and "seeking mercy of the God of heaven" in prayer.

Listening to God is an action that is nurtured in a quiet place. The Nez Perce Presbyterians know this. For the last 103 years the members of the six Presbyterian churches on the reservation in north-central Idaho have gathered for a two-week camp meeting on a tree-covered hill known as Talmaks. Every morning begins with a call to prayer. There are those who remember that the call used to come at 4 A.M. Although it now comes at 6 A.M., the first hour of the day remains devoted to prayer and worship.

I began worshiping with the Nez Perces when my dissertation studies took me to the reservation in 1994. My interest in missions to Native Americans began at Fuller Seminary and continued through my doctoral work at the University of Washington. My focus was on Native American pastors of the Presbyterian Church and the Nez Perces were second only to the Dakota in the number of ordained ministers they had produced. Since the 1887 ordination of Robert Williams, twenty individuals have been ordained as Presbyterian ministers, with a man and a woman now in seminary. The bulk of these pastors served the church at the turn of the twentieth century. I wanted to learn about what had inspired such a strong native ministry.

One of the strengths of the Nez Perce church is the ability to listen to God. The difficulty in our active lives is finding the time and granting ourselves the permission to sit long enough to pursue the voice of God. Even the first disciples had this problem. As Peter, James, and John gathered anxiously at the feet of Jesus on the Mount of Transfiguration looking for something to do, they were surprised to hear, "This is my Son, my Chosen; *listen* to him!" (Luke 9:35, RSV). God drew their attention to Jesus Christ. He needed them to stop long enough to hear what Christ had to say to them before they engaged in service for their Lord.

Steeped in an oral tradition, the Nez Perces are good listeners and have much to teach the church about prayer. It was from one of the elders that I first heard that the Creator made humankind with two ears and one mouth for a reason: that we might listen more than we talk. Prayer has sustained the Nez Perce churches for nearly two centuries and driven the evangelistic ministries of even its earliest ministers. James Hayes, ordained in 1884, traveled from the Mexican border to the Canadian border preaching among western tribes and encouraging the growth of the church. By the time of his death in 1928, he had been given an honorary doctorate from Whitworth College in recognition of his missionary work, and the Shivwit Indians of St. George, Utah, had named their church in his honor.

Asian Christians have long modeled the importance of listening to God in any kind of missionary endeavor. While visiting China in 1998 with the Cook Travel Seminar of the Presbyterian Church, my group had the pleasure of visiting a rural church outside of Hangzou. The church had just been built to accommodate the seven hundred new members who no longer fit in their older facility. At the top of the church was a prayer tower, and stacked in the corner were round woven prayer mats. When we asked about them, we were each given one and told that the church held round-the-clock prayer vigils as the church building and its membership was expanding. God raised up that church, and the congregation bore witness to God's continuing work among them.

The power of this praying people was illustrated to us when we visited a Buddhist temple. As we walked across the parking lot to our bus, our guide was demonstrating the use of a small souvenir bell for a temple ritual. Passing a diminutive woman picking up trash in the lot, our Chinese American guide was surprised to hear her say to him under her breath, "Leave those idols and follow Jesus." This woman could have faced a prison term for proselytizing. Her courage in addressing perfect strangers with the gospel was born of her certainty of God's love for her and his call to share that love with others. She knew her God and listened to him and was made strong to witness for him. She testified to Packer's words, "Knowing God gives one great energy for God."[4]

Listening to Others

The Presbyterian Church in South Korea sends more missionaries around the world than the church in the United States. It also harbors some of the largest Presbyterian congregations in the world. While there in 1998, I attended a 6 A.M. prayer meeting at the Myungsung Presbyterian Church of more than fifty thousand members. This was the third prayer meeting of the morning with two others to follow. The church was packed. This happens every morning of the week! The church in Korea knows the importance of prayer, of knowing their God and listening to him.

God told the disciples to listen to Christ because their Lord was about to put them to work—his work. The missionary God was calling his followers to mission: "The harvest is plentiful, but the laborers are few; therefore ask the Lord of the harvest to send out laborers into his harvest." It was imperative that they learn to listen and to teach others to do so:

"Whoever listens to you listens to me" (Luke 10:2, 16, NRSV). He sent them out, then, to do as he did, proclaiming the good news, healing the sick, glorifying God. "Listen to me, my people, and give heed to me, my nation," cried the Lord God (Isa. 51:4, NRSV). Listen to me, he said, and then you will be ready to listen to others.

Listening to others means being open to hearing what they are saying. It means putting oneself aside long enough to take in what another has to say, both expressed and unexpressed. It means, in Henri Nouwen's words, creating "a free space where the stranger can enter and become a friend."[5] It means learning to offer hospitality. As Anne Leo Ellis writes, it begins with listening:

> First, we must listen. Carefully, thoughtfully, without interruption, without hidden agendas, without preconceptions. Next, we need to think. And talk. With each other. As openly as possible, prepared for misunderstanding and anger, but also for healing, comprehension, reconciliation—friendship.[6]

This kind of listening is a gift of God but can be honed and enhanced by practice. My parents were Sunday school superintendents while I was in high school, and they often asked me to pick up new students and take them with me to our Sunday evening youth group. I usually dreaded these ordeals of introducing virtual strangers into the group. I didn't know what to say to them, and the twenty minutes to the church always seemed to take all evening. I can still hear my father's words: "Ask them about themselves. Listen and they will talk." It was a good exercise in learning to be hospitable, in learning to listen to others. On the mission field I would learn the value of hospitality.

When I went to Guatemala with the Christian Service Corps in 1976, it was because I had been listening to Dr. Ron Frase. Our teacher and advisor for the Latin American Theme Dorm at Whitworth College, Dr. Frase challenged us to listen to the voices of the two-thirds world. He introduced us to new faith heroes such as Dom Helder Camara, Paulo Freire, and Cesar Chavez. Our hearts were stirred to speak out against political, economic, and spiritual oppression and to stand with the marginalized. We responded with boycotts, letter-writing campaigns, and prayer vigils. And when I graduated I thought I had heard enough—I was ready for real action! I went to Guatemala on a crusade to save the oppressed Guatemalans. I was surprised to learn how little I could do (especially with my limited Spanish) besides listen!

Guatemala was one of those watershed experiences. It turned mission on its head for me. Expecting to make great strides forward in alleviating poverty and bringing in the kingdom of God, I stumbled over the language and suffered culture shock and amoebic dysentery. I soon realized that my three-year commitment would hardly allow me to learn to speak Spanish, much less make much of a difference in the face of grave political oppression and heart-rending poverty.

As a history teacher at the Inter-American School in the highlands of Quetzaltenango, I was limited in even the kind of people I encountered. A quarter of our students were missionary kids and the rest were primarily upper-class Guatemalans wanting an American education. These students were not materially deprived or oppressed. But many were spiritually impoverished and blind to the needs of those around them. Two things came of this experience: as the stranger, I learned something about hospitality as it was graciously offered to me. I also learned how God can work when we listen to him and to each other. Mission is a two-way street.

Ninfa rescued fellow teacher Jan and me from fleeing the Casa Colonial, the boarding house where we had moved to acquire more of the culture and to witness to Christ. A resident of the Casa, a medical student, and a member of the local Presbyterian church, Ninfa became our friend and interpreter of the culture. Her greatest gift to us was listening to us, gently correcting our broken Spanish with good humor, and introducing us to others. Because she spoke no English, we gained fluency in Spanish. Because she was willing to share her life with us, we gained insight into Guatemalan culture. These gifts, wrapped in the friendly, compassionate person of Ninfa, allowed Jan and me to begin to come to terms with our cultural struggles and to recognize that mission means receiving as well as giving. Claude Marie Barbour calls this "mission-in-reverse": "The minister can and should learn from the people ministered to [by] taking these people seriously [and] listening to them."[7] Tom Montgomery-Fate calls this "co-mission," which he defines as "a mutual process of risk and liberation, of co-building bridges of understanding."[8] Both insist that mission is a give-and-take relationship with those in the culture to whom we have come to minister, and a partnership in ministry with indigenous Christians within the culture.

As our friendship deepened, we encouraged one another in ministry. Ninfa was far better equipped to reach out to those in the boarding house, as she was doing before we came, than we were. So we prayed for her and her ministry and took part as she led in attending church functions and interacting with our boarding house friends. She also challenged us to turn the eyes and hearts of our students toward their compatriots in need.

By the end of our first year there, Jan and I realized that many high-schoolers had never visited a Mam or Quiché home. These local descendants of the Mayans help make up roughly half of Guatemala's population. Student awareness of them was usually limited to seeing them in the streets or markets. Ninfa suggested that we encourage student awareness and compassion for these, the marginalized in Guatemalan society. With her help and that of local Presbyterian missionaries, we took classes to visit a local Indian farmer who was working in a mission program for agricultural development. As his guests, we ate tortillas hot off the fire and drank atol, a local sweetened drink, while he demonstrated how he was teaching his neighbors to glean more from their crops and raise rabbits for extra meat. His hospitality did more to open our students' eyes to the plight of the poor and help them build relationships with them than anything we could have taught them from a textbook.

We also set up opportunities for students to make weekly trips to both a local orphanage and an old folks' home for the indigent, usually indigenous, population. Students read to the children and old ones, played games with them and sat and talked with and listened to them. In short, they made friends with these neighbors for whom they had previously had little more than contempt. As they prayed for their new friends and began to listen to God's heart for these, his people, their own faith was strengthened and they became advocates for these new brothers and sisters.

Undergirding the community awareness and outreach that we fostered at the Inter-American School was the growth of a weekly student Bible study. We encouraged "closet Christians" on campus to come together to seek the Lord, to search the scriptures and to pray for one another and one another's ministry at school and in the community. The evening gathering grew as we worked to develop student leaders who could help the group incorporate their Christian faith into their daily lives. It was exciting to see the students slowly begin to show more care and concern for one another and for others less well off. They became more hospitable.

Henri Nouwen claims that hospitality is "not to change people, but to offer them space where change can take place."[9] Mission is both giving and receiving hospitality, and all are often changed in the process. Nearly twenty years later I again experienced the kind of hospitality I had received in Guatemala. My Nez Perce brothers and sisters in their kindness and hospitality reminded me of the importance of listening to each other and so creating space to allow each other to grow in wisdom and in faith.

In the throes of doctoral dissertation deadlines and demands, I found myself running back and forth across the mountains from Seattle to the

Nez Perce reservation near Lewiston, Idaho, a number of times to gather information for my work. Somewhere in my studies the pace slowed and the focus changed. What had been a project became people with names and faces. I was drawn to the Nez Perces for longer periods of time because they became my friends. And that only happened because, in true Nez Perce fashion, they extended hospitality to me and encouraged me to sit and listen and simply be with them. Nancy, a tribal and church elder, spread out her blanket for me to sit with her in worship. Jeannie invited me to go sweating at a sweat lodge with her and that led to sharing histories, our sorrows and our joys. So many others simply invited me to slow down, sit with them, and allow the Lord to build mutually enriching relationships. The generosity and hospitality of the Nez Perces speak volumes to a church today that is too often consumed with programs, agendas, and activities that keep it from nurturing relationships that can be life-changing.

Listening alone can be life-giving. Two years ago I visited South Africa with an organization called Plowshares. We spent two weeks meeting with representatives from across the political and social spectrum to learn about the transformation in that country since the end of apartheid. Our visit to the Truth and Reconciliation Commission (TRC) was very moving. Headed by Archbishop Desmond Tutu, the TRC was a government-mandated project that sought Christian objectives of justice, forgiveness, and reconciliation following the atrocities of the era of apartheid. We met with the deputy chair, Alex Boraine, and a member of the TRC, Mary Burton. Both spoke to us of the importance of the TRC as a place where the victims of apartheid could share their stories and their suffering could be "heard, recognized and reverenced by the nation."[10]

The five-volume report (nearly three thousand pages) of the TRC was about to be turned over to the government with recommendations for reparations. It contained the stories of twenty-one thousand victims and the testimonies of seven to eight thousand perpetrators. Burton emphasized the importance of the TRC's role in listening to the victims. Commission responses were kept to a minimum as the multiracial panel listened attentively to those who spoke. The process of healing began for many when they were finally able to be heard and to share their stories. Mothers whose sons and husbands were tortured and killed, and families ripped apart by forced removals and bloody government reprisals were finally given the dignity of a compassionate hearing. Listening to another's pain allowed South Africa to acknowledge its brutal history and begin to find healing.

Learning to listen to others encourages conversation and relationship building. It allows us to be community and to engage in mission. Lesslie

Newbigin even goes so far as to claim that it is through community that we are saved. He considers Paul's query in Romans 10:14 as pivotal: "How can they believe in the one of whom they have not heard? And how can they hear without someone preaching to them?" (NIV). According to Newbigin, "there could be no salvation straight from above through the skylight, but only as we open the door to the neighbor whom God has appointed to be the bearer of salvation."[11] We become the means of God's grace for each other. Listening to one another and building friendships is key to building community where truth and love can be communicated.

Mission today has entered a new paradigm, as missiologists David Bosch, Andrew Walls, Lesslie Newbigin, and many others have well documented. We can rejoice that the Christian church is truly global in nature. Most missionaries now come from the fields in the southern and eastern hemispheres that were themselves mission fields only a generation or two ago. The biggest mission field is, perhaps, right on our doorstep. North America has not only found diverse cultures living in its own neighborhoods, but the secular society has, in Newbigin's words, become pagan. There is now more need than ever to learn to listen to each other and build relationships so that we might not only gain a hearing for the gospel, but learn what God may be saying to us through a culture not our own.

My work with Native American students at the seminary here in Dubuque continues to foster the practice of listening. At times they remind me how imperfectly I still do that! I have found it very helpful to enlist the aid of prominent Native Americans in the denomination to help me listen. I am indebted to them for their friendships and their wisdom, their love and their grace. Through them I gain sensitivity, awareness, and understanding as I walk in Native American circles. They guide and teach, encourage and engage me in mission, as Ninfa did in Guatemala. Hearing the needs, recognizing the gifts, and valuing the contributions of the Native American communities, we partner together to serve those communities by raising up pastoral leadership.

As the *missio Dei* continues to unfold in this new millennium, I remain convinced of the importance of listening—first to God and then to what he is doing in and through his world. I continue to strive for understanding, awareness, and faithful listening. When I was in Guatemala, the senior Presbyterian missionary, Stan Wick, impressed upon me that unless I sat first at Jesus' feet, I had nothing to give to God's people,. And so I remain in the Word of God and in his presence, committed to listening to him and to his people, that my heart may be both enlarged by his love for his creation and broken by the things that break the heart of God.[12] I teach this to my students, for the world desperately needs to hear and experience the good news of a risen Savior whose story isn't finished yet.

NOTES

1. David J. Bosch, *Transforming Mission: Paradigm Shifts in Theology of Mission* (Maryknoll, N.Y.: Orbis, 1991), 390.

2. Lesslie Newbigin, *The Gospel in a Pluralist Society* (Grand Rapids: Eerdmans, 1989), 133.

3. J. I. Packer, *Knowing God* (Downers Grove, Ill.: InterVarsity Press, 1973), 29.

4. Ibid., 23.

5. Henri J. M. Nouwen, *Reaching Out: The Three Movements of the Spiritual Life* (Garden City, N.Y.: Doubleday, 1975), 51.

6. Anne Leo Ellis, *First, We Must Listen: Living in a Multicultural Society* (New York: Friendship Press, 1996), 7.

7. Claude Marie Barbour, "Seeking Justice and Shalom in the City," *International Review of Mission* (July 1984): 304.

8. Tom Montgomery-Fate, *Beyond the White Noise: Mission in a Multicultural World* (St. Louis: Chalice Press, 1997), 6.

9. Nouwen, *Reaching Out,* 51.

10. Peter Storey, "A Different Kind of Justice: Truth and Reconciliation in South Africa," *Christian Century* (September 10–17, 1997): 78.

11. Newbigin, *Gospel in a Pluralist Society,* 84.

12. Tim Dearborn, *Beyond Duty: A Passion for Christ, a Heart for Mission* (Federal Way, Wash.: World Vision, 1997), 53. Dearborn quotes World Vision's founder, Bob Pierce, who said, "Let my heart be broken with the things that break the heart of God."

Growing Evangelizing Churches

*I*t was not until 1991, when Louisville Presbyterian Theological Seminary called me to become the first incumbent of the William A. Benfield Jr. Chair of Mission and Evangelism, that I began to discover that I was, and had been becoming all my life, a missiologist. It would never have happened if John Mulder, president of Louisville Seminary, had not read a book I published in 1985 dealing with the theology of evangelistic ministry, *Be My Witnesses*. He initiated the conversation that eventually resulted in this call and a change of direction for me that has since drawn together all the threads of what appears to be an unconventional pilgrimage. I explained when I came to the seminary that I would need some time to orient myself in this field, since I had been working as a college dean for several years. I faced a steep learning curve as I set out to learn the missiological literature that would be the stuff of my courses. It has been not only a fascinating intellectual challenge but a spiritual discovery to find out, as I have been teaching mission, that all my life I was, in fact, being formed for this task.

Mission and evangelism were the central focus of my own Christian formation, especially growing up at Hollywood First Presbyterian Church in California. The Great Commission was a constant challenge to us. The call to serve Christ in some form of ministry was placed before every young person coming up in that church. The large college ministry stood under the motto, "To know Christ, and to make him known." Mission and ministry were omnipresent themes. We knew "our" missionaries, supported them, hosted them, followed their stories with fascination, and looked upon them as the models we should all follow.

But we also knew that mission did not begin when one crossed the borders of America en route to a foreign country. Southern California was already a highly secularized society by the middle of the twentieth century. When our family got up on Sundays, put on our best clothes, and drove off to church, we were a noticeable minority in our neighborhood. I was aware of the fact that my school campus was a difficult mission field. My parents spent a lot of time in small group Bible study, trying to figure out what it meant to be a Christian in the worlds in which they lived. We all struggled with "witnessing," found it very hard to do, and sometimes had to contend with real guilt about how ineffective we were in our American mission field.

I had sensed a call to Christian ministry as a boy. Originally I expected to become a missionary to the South Seas (I even knew the archipelago and the island!). As I grew, the call did not weaken, but its focus changed. I realized that I was not to pick the place and function. In high school, however, I had a strong experience of calling to educational ministry, which was not as sensational as either foreign mission or the preaching ministry. But I was confident that this was what I was to do and that I needed to get a good educational foundation. Shortly after entering college (UCLA), I became a candidate for the ministry under the care of the Presbytery of Los Angeles. Upon completion of my junior year, I decided to continue my education in Europe. I wanted to strengthen my command of the German language so that I could work competently as a theologian, since I thought I would be heading eventually to Scotland, the Mecca of theological study for Presbyterians. While all of my friends went off to Princeton Seminary, I set out for Hamburg and enrolled in the theology faculty of that university.

What looked then like a detour proved to be the first step in a process that made me into a missiologist. I left Hollywood deeply aware of the importance of the faith community for my own spiritual journey, and for the carrying out of our Lord's missionary mandate. The experience of a particular church as a missional church (we would never have used that language then!) was the foundation upon which I began to build. In particular, I had been strongly influenced by the evangelistic vision of Henrietta C. Mears, whom I experienced not only as a Christian educator but as a missional strategist, especially in the six years I worked on her staff while in high school and college.

At the age of nineteen, I entered the world of European Christendom, fourteen years after the end of World War II, while it was still reeling from the division into democratic West and communist East, and sorting out the catastrophe of the twentieth century in those cultures that had called themselves Christian since the time of Constantine. What we have since come to call a "paradigm shift" was going on all around us. I was living and studying about forty miles from the Iron Curtain. The Holocaust hovered over us like a cloud that would not let us see any light on the horizon. I experienced Protestant congregations that carried forward hallowed traditions but with very little sense of community or excitement. My fellow students would rarely speak about a sense of call, for most of them had chosen the ministry simply as one of the professional options open to them as university graduates. I plunged into a theological world that was grappling with the crisis of the church in the West. We were completely caught up in the secularization of the ancient cultures of Christendom, while still living in the established church structures inherited from that history.

Christendom is a term that refers to the entire and complex structure of Christianized Europe going back to Constantine and the establishment of the Christian religion by the state. It is a way of defining the comprehensive shaping of European culture through its encounter with the Christian faith, which includes all the ways that this cultural process has reshaped, domesticated, and reduced the gospel. Although the secularization of Christendom has been emerging for four centuries, much of the tradition is, at least outwardly, intact.

In 1959 when I arrived in Hamburg, Christendom was ending, in spite of the appearance of undisturbed continuity. Its demise began when Christian Germany declared war on Christian France and Britain in 1914, and was accelerated by the brutality of World War II and the Holocaust. (For the United States, Christendom ended with the turmoil over Vietnam and the civil rights movement in the 1960s and 1970s.) This Europe that had regarded itself so self-confidently as Christian was becoming a mission field. The need to evangelize its own people was emerging as an urgent priority. But at the time, evangelization was looked upon as something done by somewhat questionable specialists, working outside the proper boundaries of the church, sometimes in tents, more often in large arenas. The church, in the meantime, was devoting itself to maintaining what it had been. For the German church this was not difficult, because its impressive institutions were supported by an equally impressive partnership with the state that generated vast amounts of tax income.

Theologically, there was little awareness that we Western Christians were actually confronted with a mission field before our doors. Our concern was to find ways to carry forward the church's legacy with integrity, which entailed, of course, translating the gospel into the language of modernity. Many of us were willing to make very great alterations in the gospel so that modernity could understand it. Others of us struggled with how to be faithful to the gospel and make it understandable to modern people, without compromising too much for the sake of success. Karl Barth was calling us to see the captivity created by "religion," to recognize how distorted God's gospel had become in the course of Christendom. But there were very few who were willing to link his critique of "religion" with the real situation of the late Christendom church, rapidly being moved into a post-Christian world.

While studying at Hamburg, I heard Lesslie Newbigin give a lecture on Trinitarian mission, on the occasion of his receiving an honorary doctorate from the theology faculty of the University of Hamburg. He became immediately a mentor from afar. His books began to reshape my own theological vision of the church, albeit slowly and subtly. Other factors were working as well. I was very fortunate to study under three theologians who took the gospel seriously, who were struggling with its implications in postwar Germany, and who were committed to the church's calling to evangelize: Leonhard Goppelt (New Testament), Hans-Joachim Kraus (Old Testament), and Helmut Thielicke (theology and ethics). As they laid the foundations of theological discipline for me, they provided much needed understanding of the course of Christendom, especially since the Enlightenment. But they did so as scholars who were skeptical about the accommodations that most of the theological world was making to modernity. They were friends and colleagues of Walter Freytag, one of the world's great missiologists, who had been a professor on the Hamburg faculty but who died suddenly shortly after I arrived. As I look back, I can see that his influence was at work in their theological scholarship and teaching.

I spent five years as a student at Hamburg, and never made it to Scotland. It was, in every way, a good fit for me, a supportive and stimulating environment in which I could pursue my interests, and, as I now see it, experience my basic formation as a theologian of the mission of the church. While still a student, I led a group of American college students on a ten-week study tour of Christian missions around the world in the summer of 1962. We encountered missionaries and indigenous church leaders at all the ports of call made by a P & O Orient Lines ship traveling from Los Angeles through Asia, the Suez Canal, and finally to Naples. In Singapore, we spoke with D. T. Niles. In the final European chapter of our trip, we encountered Stephen Neill at the World Council of Churches. The contrast between the European churches and the non-Western churches heightened my own sense of the missional crisis emerging in the "Christian West."

Until very recently, few missiologists actually studied mission in preparation for their work. Their credentials range widely. I did my doctoral work in the history of Christian higher education, focusing on the secularization of an originally Christian American college (the College of New Jersey, later Princeton University). Only much later did I realize that my preparation had actually been thoroughly missiological! To use the jargon of this guild, I was involved in a study of the missional context of Western culture. I was trying to sort out this paradigm shift from the Christendom tradition to its post-Christian phase, as that process worked itself out in higher education. When I go back now and read my research from the early 1960s (I finished my Ph.D. at Hamburg in 1964), I can see in the way conservative Presbyterianism interacted with the intellectual force of the Enlightenment in the nineteenth century a provocative case study of the emergence of the West as a mission field. Sometimes I wish that I had had then the missiological insights and interpretive approaches available to me now. But it was probably far more important that I work through these various dimensions of the end of Christendom before beginning to sort out the process in my mind. The experience of paradigm shift has preceded my learning how to describe it and my attempts to interpret it—the basic stuff now of my work as a missiologist focusing on North America and Europe as mission fields.

There were in the European churches some prophetic voices who recognized that this movement from Christendom to post-Christendom was well on its way. One of those was the youth pastor of a district of the Lutheran church of Schleswig-Holstein, on the outskirts of Hamburg. Pastor Uwe Hollm, who knew Hollywood Church and some of the people who had mentored me as a child, got in touch with me as I was finishing at Hamburg and asked me to stay in Germany and enter ministry there. His vision was clear. He saw that the established church was "confirming its young people out of the church." He wanted someone to reenter the world of these young people between fifteen and twenty and reevangelize them. To do so, one could use the avenue of religious instruction in public schools. With my degree from a German university, I was qualified to do this. The legacy of Christendom in the established church in Germany meant that I, as a pastor in the Church of Schleswig-Holstein, could enter into the public schools and teach the Christian religion as a regular subject of the curriculum. This was the doorway of opportunity for my first step in ordained ministry.

I was called by the Lutheran Church of Schleswig-Holstein, and ordained to that call by the Los Angeles Presbytery, to become the first student pastor of the district of Blankenese-Pinneberg, and I began my ministry as an evangelist disguised as a religion teacher in German *Gymnasien* (roughly the equivalent of American high schools).

The strategy worked. Using the facilities of a youth center maintained by the district, we were able to build a ministry network with these young people that involved them in retreats, study projects, group travel, Bible study, and a lot of good fellowship that focused on the building of relationships. Most of them had little or no contact with their local congregations. That was the problem—they really had been confirmed out of the church! Our ministry at the district level became their alternative congregation. Although we did not worship every Sunday, we did worship often. (One of our early ecumenical challenges was the question of my leading a Communion service as one not ordained on the basis of Lutheran confessions!) We became a functional Christian community in which young people could explore further what it meant to be a follower of Jesus Christ. Many of them engaged this search very seriously. But, as I see it now, the entire enterprise was not rooted in a setting of evangelizing congregations. It was effective communication and spiritual formation for that age group, but it did not have the capacity to relate them to the larger church with which they could continue to grow.

After three years, I returned to a call in the United States. During many later visits to Hamburg and meetings with students from that chapter of shared ministry, I have had cause to think deeply about the relationship between mission and missional church. One cannot and should not, of course, know that much about the consequences of one's work. But what I have been able to see has been sobering. It appears that only a few have continued to grapple with their Christian calling. At least one of them became a pastor. One married a pastor. Some started to study theology but gave it up before long when the church proved unsupportive of them, their interests, and their initiatives. Some entered politics in order to make some kind of difference in the world. Several became (excellent!) educators. Very few are active in the church today, although most will say that they have always looked for and longed for some continuation of the kind of fellowship we shared together. One worships in an anthroposophical congregation, the only place he has found some kind of support community.

That youth ministry in Germany was an important step in my growing understanding of the crucial importance of the evangelizing community. This was negatively illustrated by the fact that there was so little real support or even possible contact for these engaged young seekers as they moved on from our ministry. The next stages in my process of becoming a missiologist continued to test and refine my thinking. I went from Hamburg back to Los Angeles to join the pastoral leadership team of Hollywood First Presbyterian Church in the area of Christian education. After eight years away, it was an experiment to see if one can "go home again." My four years there were mixed, but basically that experience came at the right time for me, as I was trying to sort out the issues raised by my years in Europe. I moved from a highly institutional European church struggling with the issues of community and mission in a rapidly changing context to a vibrant, large American congregation with a strong sense of its mission in a very secularized context. But it was also a congregation challenged by a world changing faster than it could cope with. It was important for me to recognize that Christendom mentalities can persist in powerful ways, even when the structures of Christendom have disappeared.

Whereas in Germany, I could go into the public schools all week long and teach regular courses in religion as part of the curriculum, in the United States, the separation of church and state makes that impossible. So we had at Hollywood a highly developed system of Christian education and youth activities to provide for the spiritual formation of our young people outside of school. Hollywood Church had created over the years a dynamic and attractive kind of Christian subculture into which our members could come to retreat from the secular and often confusing world in which they lived. Our young people looked upon the church as their clan, their place to belong, and it provided them identity, focus, and support in a very difficult society for youth to navigate. Their parents expected us to protect them from the many alarming aspects of the secular culture. They would drive many miles and give generously to a church that would preserve an intact Christendom system for them on its large and well-equipped campus. Evangelism meant finding people who were already more or less compatible with the folks inside this Christian compound and inviting them in. Our primary form of witness was to "bring visitors." So if the problem in Germany was the widespread failure of the congregations to function as spiritual communities to support outreach into the world, the problem at Hollywood was the understanding of evangelization. We took our evangelistic mandate very seriously, but we equated the Christian vocation with church membership and involvement in its activities. While this is certainly an essential part of what it means to be a missional church, it was too narrow a sense of the church's missionary vocation in a world rapidly becoming a very difficult mission field.

The movement to a post-Christian world and the challenge to the church to become a different kind of evangelizing community were illustrated for me at Hollywood in several episodes. I was responsible for the Sunday school system, a large and very impressive ministry that involved 350 laypeople as teachers and officers every Sunday. I had the opportunity to work with some outstanding school educators who were willing to think with me about the particular problems of Christian formation of young people growing up in the highly secularized schools of California. We all realized that one hour a week of Sunday school was not enough, over against the hours spent in school and in front of a television set every week. One option would have been to start a private school at Hollywood Church. There were certainly room and facilities available. Many raised that as an option. Although I had always been intrigued by the possibility of Hollywood Church instituting a different kind of private school model, it was clear to me that for many reasons that would not be a viable strategy. So I spent much time with some thoughtful public school teachers and administrators looking at ways that we might partner with the public school system to provide educational opportunities for Christian young people while not removing them from the public school. There would have been some legal ways of doing this, but it was never possible to get beyond the talking stage.

I finally concluded that for many of our faithful members, the Christendom mindset was firmly in place: as long as the children and youth are in Sunday school and church one morning a week and go to camp once a year, then they have all they need to make it in a society that is fundamentally Christian anyway. Today I speak of this mindset as the 90 percent fallacy. By that I mean that most of what it means to be and act as a Christian is taken care of by virtue of the fact that one is born, raised, and educated in North America. You need only to "accept Jesus," get active in a church, and give generously, and the problem is solved. This fallacy is very comfortably ensconced in the southeastern culture I now call home, but it persists even in regions of the United States as obviously secularized as the West Coast.

There is a profound resistance among many Christians to facing the radical shift of our culture into a difficult mission field. Although they decry the many obvious evidences of secularization, particularly in the media, they are not willing to face the blunt truth that the Christian church is a minority in our context and must accept the sacrificial disciplines a minority must practice if it is to function with integrity. They want their church to provide the safe refuge of a Christendom compound for at best a few hours a week, assuming that their time in that compound will sanctify them enough to survive the rest of their lives in a society that is growing more secular but is still basically Christian.

The power of this Christendom mentality became more obvious when the alternative youth culture hit Hollywood. By the late 1960s, we were dealing with hippies and pseudohippies thronging up and down the major boulevards of Hollywood every weekend. That culture also spilled over to the beaches, where young people in Southern California had always spent their summers. Several of us at Hollywood Church became convinced that we had to shift our evangelistic strategies if we were to reach these masses of young people literally before our door. We started with some music events in the main sanctuary on Saturday evening, in which popular music was performed and interpreted from the perspective of the gospel. The response was encouraging. We moved on to initiate a coffee house ministry (the Salt Company), with a range of outreach strategies to support it: street work in Hollywood, beach outreach, halfway houses for kids in trouble, and a contemporary worship service early Sunday morning.

Many young people were reached in powerful ways. Many were mobilized to engage in missional ministry as they had never done before. Those were exciting and heady days. But they were also traumatic days for much of the membership that could not tolerate these departures from the safe shape of the Christendom compound. I will never forget the negative reaction of our own young people to the fact that so many "freaks" were now showing up on our campus, especially at the Salt Company. They let us know quickly that "they had to go to school with those freaks, and they didn't want to have to go to church with them as well." Most of their parents shared their irritation and let it be known in the church. Even the contemporary worship service (in 1970, long before the present "worship wars"!) caused problems. It took place at 8:30, so that its participants were leaving the sanctuary as the 9:30 worshipers arrived. The 9:30 crowd did not like passing these unconventional young people as they walked to their pews, and so they complained. As a result, we moved the service earlier—it became the 8:19 service.

I left Hollywood to return to Germany in 1971. It had been a good and often affirming time, but it taught me the power of the Christendom mindset that does not need a state church to function. Paradoxically, I saw the very same mentality at work in East Germany in those years. I was involved in a visitation ministry of our Southern California Presbyterian churches to sister churches in East Germany. Often traveling there twice a year, I witnessed remarkable experiences of Christian faithfulness and commitment under very hard circumstances. But I also saw repeated examples of the Christendom mentality, the commitment to the maintenance of traditions at all costs, the assignment to the church of the "religious compartment" of life, the ability to divide between the private world of Christian "values" and the public world of "objective facts." These modes of action existed in both our free churches in North America and the beleaguered churches of East Germany under a hostile regime. My formation as a missiologist had been moved along significantly as I continued to "learn by doing" that North America was a mission field, and that the church needed to become a different kind of church in this new context. Hollywood Church was struggling with that challenge in the 1960s, and its response was at best a mixed one.

My return to Germany was the result of a call to come to the Church of Württemberg as a college faculty member in a training institution that prepared men and women for the ordained diaconate. (The deacon is a second order of ordained ministry in several of the European Protestant churches.) In the province in which I served, the Karlshöhe College, in Ludwigsburg near Stuttgart, prepared men and women for youth ministry, congregational ministry (in partnership with a pastor), religious instruction in elementary schools, and social welfare work. While working on the revision of the curriculum of the college, I was learning to expand my understanding of gospel witness by the great tradition of diaconal ministry in Germany. Most of the social welfare work in Germany is done through institutions allied with the diaconal ministries of the church, and our college prepared future deacons biblically, theologically, and practically for these ministries. My German students struggled with the tension between "doing witness" and "saying witness." They clearly preferred doing, and were very hesitant about articulating their faith while helping people. This tension has continued to claim my attention. It is reflected in the United States in the often-cited dichotomy between evangelism and social justice. In the late 1980s, the Presbyterian Church (U.S.A.) even identified these two emphases as the priorities of the church. The problem is, of course, the odd understanding of evangelism that does not include social justice, and the concept of social justice that can leave out the communication of God's love in Christ as the invitation to follow him. This tension is yet another way in which the passing of Christendom leaves us in a most difficult mission field.

While in Germany, I was approached by Young Life, a nondenominational evangelistic youth ministry based in the United States, to join their newly formed training department and to work on the theological education of their staff. This was actually a secondary consequence of my helping to form a working partnership between the Church of Württemberg and Young Life, which continues up to today and has done a great deal to explore the shape of youth ministry in a post-Christian world. I ended up moving to Colorado Springs in 1976 and spent ten years, as a Presbyterian minister, working in this parachurch organization.

At Young Life I encountered the concept of "incarnational evangelism," a Christ-centered practice of evangelistic ministry that is rooted in the formation of strong and loving friendships between committed adults and teenagers. The gospel was not simply formulas or pat testimonies: it was a way of living that could be shared and into which young people could be invited. Young Life had developed a sophisticated understanding of youth culture and was, in fact, doing the missiological task of contextualizing and "indigenizing" the gospel to rapidly changing youth cultures. With many wonderful colleagues, we developed the Institute of Youth Ministries, which in partnership with Fuller Theological Seminary provided an M.A. in evangelistic youth ministry with a solid theological foundation. While developing and administering the Institute, I regularly taught the course in ecclesiology, the theology of the church's mission and ministry.

The ten years of teaching that course and of working with Young Life staff as they tried to sort out who they were in the church and what their sense of calling really meant were very productive and stimulating for my formation as a missiologist (although I still would not have used this term to describe myself). We grappled with the tensions between *church* and *parachurch,* and I tried to understand why the Christendom structures that we had inherited in North America were so helpless over against new challenges like our emerging youth cultures. I am persuaded that such parachurch organizations as Young Life have arisen largely because of the failure of the traditional church systems to respond to the new missional challenges of modernity.

As I learned more about the theology of incarnational evangelistic ministry, and even wrote a book about it (*Be My Witnesses: The Church's Mission, Message and Messengers*), I realized that there was a fundamental problem when evangelism was separated out from the evangelizing community, the congregation in a particular place. When the gospel is separated from the missionary church, it becomes necessarily private and almost exclusively vertical, focusing only on God's relationship with the individual. The central biblical emphasis upon God's love for the world calling forth a people, a community of witness and outreach, diminishes. God's mission (the *missio Dei*), which has become such a major theme in contemporary missiology, is firmly rooted biblically in God's calling, equipping, and sending out a people of witness. Ultimately, the evangelistic mandate of the church must define every dimension of the church's life and activity. Whether evangelism is reduced to one activity of a congregation symbolized by an evangelism committee, or is reduced to the sole program activity of a parachurch organization, it is always a reduction of the church's evangelistic calling. God's good news is made known through the people whose very identity is found in Jesus' calling and training them to be disciples and to continue his ministry as his servants and witnesses. Mission defines the very nature of the church, and evangelization is its core and center. (This is the argument I have tried to make in my most recent book, *The Continuing Conversion of the Church*).

My somewhat surprising move to Whitworth College to become vice president for academic affairs and dean of the faculty was, as it turned out, the final step toward my discovery that I was a missiologist. The wonderful and committed faculty at Whitworth took the mandate to be a Christian liberal arts college very seriously. From the perspectives of their various disciplines, they were engaging the intellectual challenge of late modernity—the movement out of Christendom and the uncertainties of Christian vocation in a post-Christian world. At the outset of our time together, we read and discussed Newbigin's revolutionary little book, *The Other Side of 1984: Questions for the Churches*. That publication initiated the Gospel and Our Culture movement in Britain in the early 1980s, which by the end of the decade had spread to North America. At Whitworth, my colleagues taught me about the implications of the emerging critique of the Enlightenment in all our disciplines. We asked about the power of the Newtonian-Cartesian assumptions that guided Western thinking, and began to explore the powerful and threatening skepticism of *postmodernity*. But we did so as an academic community persuaded of the truth of the gospel, the faithfulness of God, and the concrete ethical significance of our calling to be witnesses to that good news. There could have been no better preparation for the unexpected but very happy discovery, at the age of fifty-one, that I was a missiologist.

There have been several important serendipities that have accompanied my movement into the formal teaching of missiology. The most important one is the recognition, summarized in what I have written above, that God's faithfulness toward me has taken concrete shape in the way each of these events has contributed to what I am now to do as a teacher of the church. I have discovered that missiology is an integrative discipline in very exciting ways. Sometimes I say that it is an obnoxious discipline, because it must move across the boundaries of our theological compartments and "get into everyone's business." Missiologists must, of necessity, work biblically, historically, systematically, ethically, practically—and in constant interaction with a whole range of social and behavioral disciplines. The focus of missiology is the church's missionary vocation as it is rooted in scripture, develops through history, is expressed more or less adequately in doctrine, and practiced in ministry and witness. I am persuaded that the center of the discipline must be the confessing, witnessing, faith-exploring particular community of faith—what we call "the local congregation." Everything we do theologically must in some way or another serve the continuing formation of mission communities for the vocation of being witnesses to Jesus Christ. That means that the preparation of pastoral leadership for such congregations must focus on the common calling of the church to mission and the particular ways in which ministers of the Word are used by God to form communities to be obedient to that calling. In the terms of Ephesians 4:11, this means that the ministry of the word will always have to be apostolic, prophetic, evangelistic, pastoral, and teaching. Only when that is happening will the saints be equipped for the work of ministry and the body of Christ be built up.

At Louisville Seminary (1991–1997) I developed a basic curriculum in mission and evangelism. A sabbatical made it possible for me to move beyond my first attempt to work theologically on evangelism, and I started the *Continuing Conversion* manuscript, which finally appeared in 2000. At the same time, I became involved in the Gospel and Our Culture Network, which has directed my attention especially to the distinctive challenges of North America as a mission field. Our research project, "Missional Church," was an attempt to encourage the broader discussion of the church's "sentness" as a witnessing community in the changing context of North America. In both of these projects, the centrality of the congregation, the evangelizing community, has become a pressing issue for me.

Columbia Seminary invited me to the Peachtree Chair of Evangelism and Church Growth with the understanding that I could specialize as a missiologist on the particular challenges of North America (and the North Atlantic legacy, i.e., Christendom) and the missional reorientation of the church in this context. With the full support of my colleagues and the administration, I have been invited to develop the Peachtree Chair around the theme of "growing evangelizing churches." This, it appears to me, is the central definition of the church in the New Testament: communities that embody good news, make Jesus Christ known, and invite neighbors to join in a pilgrimage of witness and expectation as obedient servants of the Lord Jesus Christ. The missional church understands itself as the first fruit, sign, and agent of the inbreaking reign of God that Jesus Christ proclaims and is.

Congregations that evangelize are congregations that are constantly being evangelized. This means, of course, that evangelization is about a lot more than "accepting Jesus." It is the continuing process of gospel encounter that draws communities together around Jesus Christ as their present Lord and sends them out as his witnesses. Continuing evangelization is what Paul means when he implores his churches to lead their life worthy of the calling to which they are called (1 Thess. 2:11; Phil. 1:27; Eph. 4:1). Such a process of ongoing evangelization means that every congregation is required to grapple with its conformities, the ways in which its gospel is reduced and domesticated so that it functions in captivity to its culture. The conversion that must happen is a transformation by the renewal of the mind (Rom. 12:2). This means that every minister of the Word, every teaching elder must be an evangelist—which is precisely why Ephesians 4:11 puts the "evangelist" at the center of the list of functions that are essential for the equipping of the saints. For me, this means that, as a teacher of theology, my calling is to be an evangelist in the seminary classroom. As every missionary can confirm, the witness to the gospel always transforms the witness first as it reaches out and by God's grace touches others.

Growing evangelizing congregations is the biblical strategy for God's mission. The missiologist teaching in a seminary will focus upon the formation of pastors as evangelists so that they will in turn be God's instruments, with others, to evangelize congregations, so that, in Paul's words, "grace, as it extends to more and more people, may increase thanksgiving, to the glory of God" (2 Cor. 4:15, NRSV).

Glossary of Terms

Some terms used by the professors of mission in this book may not be familiar, or they may be used here in ways that are unfamiliar. What follows are brief explanations of these terms. See noted pages for relevant uses of each term.

Christendom, post-Christian
In the fourth century the emperor Constantine declared Christianity to be the official religion of the empire. From that time until well into the twentieth century, Christianity played a normative and dominant role in Western civilization. This is referred to as *Christendom.* It is now common to refer to our era as *post-Christian,* meaning that it can no longer be assumed that Christianity is the predominant religious force shaping culture. (See Guder, pages 135–38, 140–42, 146.)

contextualization
The gospel is one. Yet the gospel must be proclaimed and celebrated in ways that are uniquely appropriate to each particular culture and context. *Contextualization* involves discovering the temporal forms (language, rituals, common life, conversation patterns) that will best express the eternal reality of the gospel in any given context. (See Haney, page 85; Wickeri, page 97.)

ecumenical
We may be Presbyterians, Methodists, Pentecostals, or Roman Catholics, but we know ourselves to be part of a much larger family, the body of Christ in the world. *Ecumenical* refers to that larger worldwide family. Thus, ecumenical ministries involve Christians of different churches joining together to bear witness to Christ, and the ecumenical movement promotes unity and cooperation among Christians. (See Rhee, page 72; Wickeri, pages 101–3; Haney, page 87.)

evangelism, evangelical
From the Greek *evangelion,* meaning "good news" or "gospel." *Evangelism* refers to the art of sharing the gospel. *Evangelical* is typically used to refer to a person (or community) for whom sharing the gospel is of utmost importance. (See Adeney, pages 16–17; Guder, pages 144–45; Skreslet, pages 66–67.)

globalization
Sometimes *globalization* refers generally to the importance of nurturing a global perspective. Currently, however, *globalization* is usually used to refer to a complex and ambiguous phenomenon in our world. Rapid technological advances and the expansion of market capitalism have combined to create this phenomenon of globalization, which one writer defines as "the extension of the effects of modernity to the entire world, and the compression of time and space, all occurring at the same time." (Robert J. Schreiter, *The New Catholicity: Theology between the Global and the Local.* New York: Orbis Books, 1997) (See Wickeri, pages 105, 107.)

missio Dei
Latin for "God's mission." *Mission* is defined as "the act or an instance of sending." In Christian mission, it is God who is the sender. The term *missio Dei* reminds us that mission does not "belong" to human beings or to our institutions. This is obvious, yet easy to forget. In mission, the church seeks to be faithful to God. Thus, the church exists for the sake of mission. We must guard against the human tendency to view mission as an activity that exists for the sake of the church. (See Lewis, page 124; George, page 42.)

missionary, mission coworker, missioner, fraternal worker
The fundamental mission dynamic is unchanging. God is the sender. The church is sent into the world in God's name. The church, in one vital aspect of mission, sets apart particular individuals to cross boundaries of geography and culture for the purpose of "sharing the gospel, and doing those deeds in the world that point beyond themselves to the new reality in Christ" (G-3.0400, *Book of Order*, Presbyterian Church (U.S.A.)).

While the fundamental mission dynamic does not change, the world does change. Thus, every generation of Christians seeks "to present the claims of Jesus Christ" (ibid., G-3.0300) in ways that are appropriate to the present moment in history. As the Christian movement has increasingly become a global reality, less and less dominated by Western churches, the church has used these various terms to identify those who cross geographical and cultural boundaries in Christ's name. (See Adeney, page 17; Skreslet, page 61; Sunquist, page 119; Wickeri, page 98.)

missional church
The noun *mission* has been turned into an adjective, *missional,* to describe a church that puts mission engagement at the very center of its life as a church. (See George, page 135; Guder, pages 135, 146.)

missiology, missiological, missiologist
In the academic world, the study of mission is called *missiology.* The person who engages in this study is a *missiologist.* The corresponding adjective is *missiological.* There is an American Society of Missiology, in which most of the Presbyterian professors of mission participate, that publishes a quarterly journal of articles about mission entitled *Missiology.* (See Guder, page 135; Skreslet, page 60; Haney, pages 79–80, 81.)

mutuality in mission
All who serve in Christ's name are both givers *and* receivers; teachers *and* learners. The term *mutuality* reminds us that mission is never a one-way street. (See Lewis, page 129; Sunquist, page 121–23; George, page 43.)

partnership, partners
During the second half of the twentieth century it became common to speak of *partnership in mission* as a way to recognize that all churches, big or small, rich or poor, northern, southern, eastern, or western, are called to work together as equals in God's mission in the world. When U.S. Presbyterians refer to "our global partners," we usually mean our colleagues from churches in other countries and regions of the world. (See Adeney, page 17; George, page 44; Skreslet, page 67.)

Presbyterian Church (U.S.A.) or PC(USA)
The writers of this volume all teach in theological seminaries affiliated with the *Presbyterian Church (U.S.A.),* abbreviated as *PC(USA).* Many have also served the PC(USA) in other leadership capacities, including mission service. Its predecessor denominations, the Presbyterian Church in the United States (PCUS) and the United Presbyterian Church in the United States of America (UPCUSA), are also mentioned.